Journeys
OUT OF
HOMELESSNESS

Journeys
OUT OF
HOMELESSNESS

THE VOICES OF LIVED EXPERIENCE

Jamie Rife,
Donald W. Burnes,
and Contributors

LYNNE
RIENNER
PUBLISHERS

BOULDER
LONDON

Published in the United States of America in 2020 by
Lynne Rienner Publishers, Inc.
1800 30th Street, Boulder, Colorado 80301
www.rienner.com

and in the United Kingdom by
Lynne Rienner Publishers, Inc.
Gray's Inn House, 127 Clerkenwell Road, London EC1 5DB

Library of Congress Cataloging-in-Publication Data
Names: Rife, Jamie, author. | Burnes, Donald W., author.
Title: Journeys out of homelessness : the voices of lived experience /
    Jamie Rife, Donald W. Burnes.
Description: Boulder, Colorado : Lynne Rienner Publishers, Inc., [2020] |
    Includes bibliographical references and index.
Identifiers: LCCN 2019024923 | ISBN 9781626378537 (hardcover) | ISBN
    9781626378605 (paperback)
Subjects: LCSH: Homelessness—United States—Case studies. | Homeless
    persons—United States—Case studies.
Classification: LCC HV4505 .R54 2020 | DDC 362.5/92092273—dc23
LC record available at https://lccn.loc.gov/2019024923

British Cataloguing in Publication Data
A Cataloguing in Publication record for this book
is available from the British Library.

Printed and bound in the United States of America

∞   The paper used in this publication meets the requirements
    of the American National Standard for Permanence of
    Paper for Printed Library Materials Z39.48-1992.

5   4   3   2   1

*To everyone with lived experience
of homelessness*

Contents

Acknowledgments

In 2016, Dave DiLeo and Don Burnes coedited and contributed chapters to *Ending Homelessness: Why We Haven't, How We Can.* One of the chapter contributors was a woman who had experienced homelessness. Her work with Don as a professional colleague and her story in that volume reinforced Don's understanding of the importance of listening to individuals with lived experience, people who could help us better understand what homelessness is really about.

Some months after the publication of *Ending Homelessness*, Don met a member of the faculty at the University of Denver who had been referred to him by a mutual acquaintance as someone he should get to know. As he walked to her office, he had no idea what to expect. An hour and a half later, after she told him her story of her time as a child living through homelessness, he was stunned. He told her that she should write it down because it was so important, so full of passion and compassion, so incredible. In a moment of unbridled enthusiasm, he even said, "Your story should be the cornerstone of a new book." That was the beginning of *Journeys out of Homelessness: The Voices of Lived Experience.*

Shortly thereafter, in discussing the idea with our publisher, Lynne Rienner said, "This book has to be more than a bunch of stories about people experiencing homelessness. There are numerous collections of that kind. You need something different." That led the two of us to focus on not only the experience of homelessness but also on the factors that were important in helping our contributors escape the ravages of homelessness, a piece of the puzzle that previously had not been given much attention.

This is not *our* book. It is the culmination of the efforts of many people, without whom the book would have remained only an idea. The real heroes and heroines of this work are the contributors to nine of the subsequent chapters. We can only express our deepest gratitude to these remarkable people. They have lived through bouts of homelessness and managed to work through them in amazing fashion. We owe so much to all of them.

In addition, we want to thank Kevin Adler. His work on Miracle Messages is one of the very bright spots in the San Francisco homelessness scene, and it's expanding beyond a local effort. We discuss his work in the concluding chapter, along with its impact. We also would like to express our gratitude to Kristin Myers for her review and contributions to Chapters 5 and 6 regarding foster care.

We couldn't be more grateful to our publisher. Lynne Rienner, of Lynne Rienner Publishers (LRP), was instrumental in helping the two of us develop the basic framework for our book and has been very supportive throughout. Her staff, including Sally Glover, Nicole Moore, and Shena Redmond, have been especially helpful, and the remaining staff at LRP have been unfailingly efficient and pleasant. Our appreciation also goes to our copyeditor, Jennifer Top. Thank you all.

Finally, I, Don, want to thank my wife, Lynn, for her extreme patience during the entire process and for her valuable contributions to various chapters. I have been able to maintain my sanity throughout the development of the book only because of her constant encouragement and support. The book wouldn't have happened without her. Many thanks, Love.

And, I, Jamie, would like to thank my dear husband, Aki, for his support and understanding. When I doubted I could do this, he encouraged me. When I grappled with decisions, he listened to me. And, when I dedicated countless hours away from him, he understood. Without him, I would not have the courage to pursue so many of the seemingly insurmountable achievements in my life. Aki, you're the best partner I could ask for, and I love and appreciate you.

It is our fervent hope that by exploring these various stories and by considering the implications that we have drawn from them, you will develop a better understanding of homelessness. As we hope we demonstrate, having to live without a home of one's own creates incredible pressures and trauma for those who must go through that experience, but for most of our contributors, there was a light at the end of the proverbial tunnel, a way out of the tragedy of homelessness. In fact, their ability to move beyond homelessness gives us hope that others can also find a way out. But, as we show, in response to this tragedy, we must be creative in developing new policies and programs to address the issue; we must think outside the box. It is our belief that focusing on natural supports and building community may well be a crucial step in that direction.

—*Jamie Rife and Donald W. Burnes*

1

Journeys out of Homelessness

To date, there has been a significant amount of literature written on the issue of homelessness, providing valuable insight, data, and in-depth research on this topic. Some of this work is qualitative in nature, including ethnographies and third-person accounts of life without a home.[1] Additionally, quantitative research, consisting of demographic and epidemiological data, outcome information, and thoughtful solutions, has added to our understanding.[2] Recent publications by the US Interagency Council on Homelessness (2018a, 2018b, 2018c, 2019) have specifically advocated for the increased use of such quantitative research. In a few cases, these two types of methodologies have been married to capture the experience of homelessness while providing implications and solutions (Wagner, 2018; Wasserman & Clair, 2010).[3]

However, one of the gaps in the current literature on homelessness, and the voice far too often absent in the discussion on how to solve homelessness, is the voice of individuals with lived experience. While it is valuable to shed light on their journeys in third person, as has been done by a number of researchers previously, this book instead provides an opportunity to hear directly from those affected by homelessness, as the contributors provide their own first-person accounts.

This book differs from others on the topic in another important way. Instead of focusing solely on the causes of homelessness and the experience of being without a home, this book asks the questions, how have individuals gotten through their experiences of homelessness, and what are the factors that were particularly important in assisting them in becoming housed? Exploring how these nine individuals were able to move through homelessness provides guidance for policymakers, service providers, and others who are working to end homelessness.

We also strive to humanize an issue seen by most as abstract, a population of individuals largely ignored by society. For the average American, simply hearing the statistics on the magnitude of homelessness can lead to feeling overwhelmed. Additionally, even when informed on the issue, most have no idea where to start to make a difference; it seems insurmountable. In fact, the issue is not. Therefore, we seek in this book to assist readers in understanding the issue from both a historical and a research perspective—and seeing that homelessness is a solvable issue.

Although some readers may be inspired by the stories of resiliency contained within these covers, resiliency should not be confused with a solution. Homelessness has much deeper, more fundamental root causes that need to be addressed, evidenced by the current scale of the phenomenon in the United States. It is a result of systemic failings, not personality flaws, as illustrated throughout the contributors' stories.

What Is Homelessness?

To fully understand the issue of homelessness, one must first understand the term *homeless*. The word, at its root, literally means not having a home. In defining *home* themselves, the contributors used words and phrases such as: (1) a safe, secure, stable place; (2) no place I'd rather be; (3) home is my castle; (4) a place to keep all my stuff; (5) a place where I have some control over my environment; and (6) a place to build relationships. Therefore, in part, "homeless" can refer to a lack of these conditions.

Terms related to safety, stability, and security provide some insight into why this issue can cause such deep trauma. Safety and security are two of human beings' most fundamental needs. Without having these two essential needs met, it is difficult to grow and flourish as a member of society.

It is also important to note the adverse reaction many of the contributors had to the very term *homeless*. This, in large part, is due to the stereotypical images the term conjures up for the average person and the stigma these images create. Contributors preferred various different phrasings, as seen throughout their chapters.

The Federal Definitions of Homelessness

One of the fundamental aspects of understanding homelessness is the variance between US federal agencies in how they define the issue. There are two overarching definitions utilized in the field, the first of which is used by the US Department of Education (USED) and, consequently, public schools throughout the country. Section 725(2) of the McKinney-Vento Homeless Assistance Act defines "homeless children and youths" as individuals who lack a fixed, regular, and adequate nighttime residence.

According to the USED definition, children must have a place they can go each night, not subject to change, that meets their safety and security needs. Protections under the educational definition of homelessness provide children and youth attending public school a particular set of federal rights to encourage school stability, something crucial for social and academic success.

Yet, the parents or guardians of these students, or even independent youth themselves, do not necessarily qualify for housing assistance as they may not meet the criteria for the US Department of Housing and Urban Development (HUD) definition of homelessness; this fact is one of the systemic difficulties in addressing root causes of homelessness. In many instances, the US Department of Education recognizes a family as living in a homeless situation, making them eligible for certain services, even though they do not meet the narrower definition of "literally homeless" under HUD and thus do not qualify for housing support, potentially leaving these children, youth, and families in a never-ending cycle of instability.

The most significant difference between the two definitions is the inclusion of those who are "doubled up" in the USED definition—individuals or families who are unable to maintain their own housing and are forced to live with different family members, friends, or others—but are generally excluded from the HUD definition. The doubled up are also recognized by the US Department of Health and Human Services (National Health Care for the Homeless Council, 2018); however, this population of those experiencing homelessness is generally not eligible for housing assistance, a loophole that leaves many, particularly families with children, in what one of the book's contributors refers to as the "in-between."

For the purposes of this book, all contributors met at least one of the federal definitions of homelessness. Some of them were "literally homeless," according to HUD's definition. Many of them also resided in places unfit for habitation, were doubled up, spent time in motels, or were homeless unaccompanied youth, bouncing from place to place.

Descriptors of Homelessness

Ever since its rise to public prominence in the late 1970s and early 1980s, researchers and writers have used diverse ways to describe this complex phenomenon. One of the most common is to define the issue in terms of various subpopulations: single adults, both men and women; families with children; families without children; veterans; youth and young adults; victims of domestic violence; seniors; and by race and ethnic background as well.

Starting with the seminal work of Dennis Culhane, Stephen Metraux, and others, a second set of descriptors has focused on length of time homeless (Culhane, Metraux, & Hadley, 2002; Culhane, Metraux, Park, Schretzman, & Velente, 2007). Now, according to Tobin and Murphy, "Most researchers use a typology that classifies homeless experiences as 'transitional, episodic, or chronic'" (2016, p. 39). Those whose experience of homelessness is transitional find themselves in that predicament for a single, relatively brief period of time. Others cycle in and out, experiencing a few episodes of homelessness. Chronics are defined as experiencing an episode of homelessness lasting over a year or having four episodes over the past three years. In addition, for a person to be classified as experiencing chronic homelessness, he or she must also have some type of disability. As Tobin and Murphy indicate, this typology has now become commonplace, and federal policy during the last twenty years has taken it to heart, focusing primarily on those experiencing chronic homelessness, including those who have served in the military.

Another typology of homelessness comes from the work of Teresa Gowan (2010). She divides the population into those described as "sin-talk," "sick-talk," and "system-talk." In their analysis of Gowan's work, Whelley and McCabe indicated that "these apt terms clarify the three dominant frameworks for understanding the causes of homelessness: the independent agency perspective, the individualized medical (medicalized) perspective, and the structural perspective" (2016, p. 207). Those who fall into the sin-talk category experience homelessness because they are somehow deficient, deviant, and/or have made bad choices. The medicalized perspective blames homelessness on the pathology or pathologies of the individual. According to the system-talk perspective, homelessness is caused by systemic/structural factors.

Whelley and McCabe (2016) added a fourth category to Gowan's typology, namely, "structure plus."

> In reality, individual free will, myriad pathologies, and systemic factors intersect and combine to explain the causes of homelessness. . . . Nor will one solution to homelessness emerge from such a combined perspective; structural elements must be addressed, but services should be molded to fit individual needs rather than being prescribed by service professionals, private agencies, public funding, or government agencies. (pp. 208–209)

Wasserman and Clair (2016), in describing their earlier work (2010), indicated that service agencies, particularly those associated with religious organizations, provide services that can be distinguished as working with sinners, working with the meek, and working for social justice (2016, p. 126).

The Extent of Homelessness

Data on the extent of homelessness in the United States vary between agencies, which creates large discrepancies in the reported numbers of individuals experiencing homelessness. The inclusion of the doubled up in the USED definition, and the exclusion of it from the HUD definition except under narrow circumstances, is the main cause for this discrepancy in annual reports. However, it is important to understand the breadth of the issue by examining both sets of data. The discrepancy between these two definitions also leads to unfortunate circumstances for those doubled up, as we will discuss in Chapter 4.

Public School Data

Each year public schools across the United States report on the number of enrolled students who are identified as experiencing homelessness. As of school year 2015–2016, the most recent data available, over 1.3 million children experienced homelessness (National

Center for Homeless Education, 2017a). That means approximately 2.5 percent of our nation's students do not have a fixed, regular, adequate nighttime residence. This number does not include their parents or guardians, or younger or older siblings not currently enrolled in school. If one adds in older and younger siblings and single adults and adult couples, we estimate there may be as many as 3.5–4 million persons experiencing homelessness across the United States, using the USED definition.

Approximately 14.4 percent of those 1.3 million homeless children resided in shelters or transitional housing, or they were awaiting foster care. Another 3.3 percent were unsheltered, meaning they were living in cars, parks, campgrounds, temporary trailers, or abandoned buildings; another 6.5 percent were living in hotels or motels due to a lack of adequate alternative accommodations. That leaves another 75.8 percent of children and families in doubled-up situations (National Center for Homeless Education, 2018). These families technically have a physical roof under which to sleep; however, these children may not have a bed, a quiet place to complete homework, or space to even unpack their belongings, or their entire family may be living in one bedroom. They have no lease, ownership, or control over their environment and are at the mercy of those with whom they reside. These situations are most often temporary, causing a family or child to bounce between multiple relatives or friends, certainly far from the "fixed" circumstances that the USED definition includes. Sometimes these living situations are also unsafe. Having a roof does not constitute having a home, as many of these families and their children are often less stable and less safe than those who meet the HUD definition of homelessness.

Included in this count were over 111,000 unaccompanied homeless youth identified, or those students experiencing homelessness while not in the physical custody of a parent or guardian during the 2015–2016 school year (National Center for Homeless Education, 2017b). Familial dysfunction is reported by unaccompanied youth as the primary reason for their leaving the home, including substance abuse, pregnancy, sexual orientation, sexual activity, aging out of foster care, and parental abuse. Additionally, these students are often left in a homeless situation due to the deportation, incarceration, illness, or death of their parent or guardian (National Center for Homeless Education, 2017c). These young people constitute one of our nation's most vulnerable populations; however, little attention and few resources are dedicated to them.

HUD Data

Even by HUD's narrower definition, the numbers of individuals experiencing homelessness are astounding. Each January, a national Point-in-Time (PIT) count is conducted in an attempt to estimate a deduplicated number of individuals experiencing homelessness. There are several limitations to this methodology (for an in-depth discussion of these, see O'Brien, 2016). While the efficacy of this method is debated regularly, it is the current standard for data collection and the basis for the Annual Homeless Assessment Report (AHAR) to Congress. In 2017, according to the PIT count, 553,742 individuals in the United States were homeless. This was the first time in seven years that the number had increased, largely fueled by increases in a handful of major cities. Family homelessness constituted 33 percent of that number, meaning 184,661 families with children were experiencing HUD's version of homelessness. Additionally, another 40,799 were unaccompanied youth, or individuals under the age of twenty-five not in the custody of a parent or guardian. Perhaps most shocking about these data is that while approximately 35 percent of the overall homeless population in the United States is unsheltered, among unaccompanied youth, this number rises to 55 percent (US Department of Housing and Urban Development, 2017a).

Trends in these data over time reflect the shifting demographics in our nation. The narrative of the panhandler on the street corner is not representative of this population, as you will see in subsequent chapters. Instead, a larger percentage of individuals counted during the PIT consists of women, families, children, and youth.

While the data demonstrate a growing need for concern, within these numbers lies proof that targeted efforts and adequate resourcing can make a substantial impact. A national and federal focus on ending veteran homelessness led to a decrease of 46 percent in the number of homeless veterans between 2010 and 2017 (US Department of Housing and Urban Development, 2017a). Nationally, a growing list of communities has statistically ended veteran homelessness, fueled by an infusion of resources, coordinated efforts, robust data, and support across sectors (US Interagency Council on Homelessness, 2018a). These efforts demonstrate that ending homelessness is in fact feasible with adequately resourced systems, coordinated solutions, and shared responsibility. If it can be done for veterans, it can be done for others as well.

Personal Versus Systemic
Causes of Homelessness

There is a raging debate in this country about the causes of homelessness. Some argue that people become homeless as a result of personal problems, issues, or flaws. For example, Baum and Burnes suggested in *A Nation in Denial* (1993), based on a review of over 100 accounts and epidemiological studies, that a substantial majority of those experiencing homelessness suffer from untreated substance addiction and/or untreated mental illness, and they were widely criticized for being "neoliberal." Those who contend that personal issues cause homelessness point to data about the extent of mental illness, alcoholism, and drug addiction among those experiencing homelessness, and they argue that many of those without homes choose to be there. This perspective can be summarized as follows: individuals experiencing homelessness are either unmotivated, battling mental illness, struggling with alcohol or drug addiction, or in the situation due to a series of bad choices, including choosing to be homeless.

Others argue that homelessness generally is caused by a series of systemic factors over which individuals have little or no control. William Ryan, in his influential book *Blaming the Victim* (1976), argued that focusing on personal characteristics of those experiencing homelessness equates to blaming the victims of systemic forces. Additionally, there are *many more* housed persons who are unmotivated, battling mental illness, and struggling with alcohol or drug addiction, and who among us has never made a bad decision? Furthermore, except for a miniscule handful, data clearly show people do not choose the life of stigma, shame, rejection, and precariousness.

What, then, distinguishes between those who are housed and those who are not? The simple answer is resources: financial, housing, employment, nutritional, health care, childcare, educational, and transportation—that is, the resources needed to maintain some level of self-sufficiency and stability. These resources also include human resources, social capital, people who care, networks of support, a community on which to rely. We will discuss all of these in more detail in subsequent chapters.

For those who lean toward more systemic causes, it is true that homelessness can be traced to one word: poverty, both economic and social—a lack of resources. This dearth of resources can be credited to a number of systemic factors that are beyond individual control. There is a lack of adequate affordable housing, significant unemployment, underemployment, low wages, inadequate health care and health insurance, inadequate childcare, food insecurity and food deserts, lack of access to education, and inadequate transportation. Racial discrimination reinforces all of these inadequacies, and all are aggravated by times of national economic distress, such as the Great Recession, and by growing economic inequality. Added together, these factors push many people into homelessness. (For an extended discussion of these and other forces, see Burnes & DiLeo, 2016).

In addition, there is the large cohort of individuals in extreme poverty who are at risk of becoming homeless. A recent study indicated that almost half of the randomly selected respondents in the United States would have to borrow to pay an unexpected expense of $400 (Board of Governors of the Federal Reserve System, 2017). Individuals experiencing homelessness and people in extreme poverty simply cannot borrow money. In short, we have not figured out a way to prevent homelessness due to the underlying issue of poverty.

Homelessness and Public Opinion

Four Hundred Years of Homelessness

To understand the current state of public opinion on homelessness, it is important to first look briefly at this issue's history. Many Americans seem to believe that homelessness in this country is a relatively new phenomenon caused by regressive governmental policies and the recessions that have plagued this country over the last forty years. The truth is that homelessness is not new. Throughout our history, people have lived on the margins. Starting in the earliest days of the colonies, Americans have viewed these individuals and families variously as a threat to their young society that was relegated to the poorhouses and almshouses made famous by the English; as the penniless immigrants who arrived on our shores in waves; as heroic rugged individuals forging west to open the frontier; as the wounded and bitter soldiers and freed slaves of the Civil War and its aftermath; as the hoboes who rode the recently constructed rails and lived in the shantytown hobohemias; as the destitute victims of the Great Depression; as the shameful derelicts of skid row; and, finally, as today's "new homeless." By the late 1970s, we were confronted with a growing surge of those experiencing homelessness, and the public consciousness of this phenomenon was raised, fueled in part by the very public displays of homelessness advocacy by such individuals as Mitch Snyder and Carol Fennelly of the Community for Creative Non-Violence.

Despite the debate about the causes of this huge influx of the destitute among us, there can be no denying the importance of several factors. The huge growth in the overall US population—the Baby Boom—and its maturation in the late 1960s and 1970s meant that there were millions more people prone to the conditions created by inadequate housing, un-/underemployment, and the challenges for persons with substance abuse disorders or those grappling with mental illness.

Major and well-intended federal policies also unintentionally expanded the number of homeless. The deinstitutionalization of individuals diagnosed with a mental illness from state hospitals started in the Kennedy and Johnson years and left many former patients and inmates of state hospitals without housing and services, as the needed supply of community mental health facilities never materialized. The decriminalization of public intoxication left many public inebriates without shelter as former "drunk tanks" were never replaced by the necessary public detox facilities. Urban renewal and the destruction of skid rows dispersed those without a home throughout urban areas where their needed services, including housing and jobs, were very slow, if ever, to materialize. The Reagan administration oversaw significant cutbacks in funding for housing and other reductions in benefits for the very poor among us, and many of these cutbacks continue today. More recently, welfare reform, one of the signature accomplishments of the Clinton presidency, has reduced benefits for many poor families, forcing them either into homelessness or, at the very least, into utilizing services intended for the homeless. Finally, the recent Great Recession devastated many families, forcing them into foreclosure and then into battles for rental units, into emergency shelters and transitional housing, or onto the streets.

As the United States has struggled with its attitudes toward the homeless and how to help them, endless debates, repeated by each successive generation, have been fueled by a cycle of pity, distaste, fear, anger, and helplessness felt by all, rich and poor, when there is impoverishment, homelessness, and destitution in our midst. The questions remain the same: Should services provide direct financial assistance, or should they provide shelter? Should policies force the homeless into institutions or respect their freedom and right to self-determination? Should the help be compassionate and generous, or should it exercise social control by rewarding work and industry while punishing idleness and intemperance? Should assistance be an entitlement paid for by the general public through taxes, or should it be available only when it has been earned by work? Should helping the homeless be the responsibility of government, or should the primary source of help be private charitable organizations? The answers to all these questions have always depended on the definition of who is worthy of assistance and who is not. (For a more extensive examination of the history of homelessness, see Chapters 6 and 7 in Baum & Burnes, 1993).

The Perception Gap

The central organizing theme throughout the history of homelessness in the United States has been the distinction between the "deserving" and the "undeserving" poor. Those who are deserving of our help are those whose housing circumstances are beyond their individual control, who are experiencing homelessness through no fault of their own. The undeserving are those whose homelessness is a direct consequence of something they have done to produce that result.

Rollinson and Pardeck (2006), in analyzing the worthy and the unworthy, indicated that the underpinnings of this unfortunate distinction can be traced back to religious roots. In comparison with much of Europe, where religious values and beliefs were tied closely to what the authors called the "Catholic ethic," US values have been tied more closely to a "Calvinistic ethic" that focuses on work and the "laziness" of the poor (p. 81). The authors went on to argue that these underlying values have significant implications for the way that countries think about and address the issue of homelessness.

The corollary to the distinction between deserving and undeserving is that those deemed undeserving do not generate public sympathy. Therefore, a fundamental solution to homelessness may lie in shifting perceptions of who is deserving or undeserving by addressing commonly held misconceptions about who experiences homelessness in this country and whether it derives from personal or systemic reasons.

Such misconceptions are, at one level, understandable. For most Americans, their only direct contact with homelessness comes from the individuals they actually see (i.e., panhandlers on street corners at traffic lights; individuals lying on sidewalks, in doorways, or in alleys; people walking along talking to or yelling at their unseen voices; or the prototypic bag ladies or gents, pushing shopping carts loaded with all their worldly possessions). These are the *visible* individuals experiencing homelessness, and, unfortunately, they reinforce the negative stereotypes. Many assume that they represent the total population of those without a home.

However, based on PIT and AHAR data, it is clear that they represent only about 15–20 percent of the total homeless population (Metro Denver Homeless Initiative, 2017; US Department of Housing and Urban Development, 2017a). The rest consist of families with children, runaway or throwaway youth, people in shelters and transitional housing, people who work but do not earn enough to afford housing, members of the LGBTQ community, and others who are afraid to be seen. They are the *invisible* ones, and they make up the vast majority of the total population of persons experiencing homelessness.

Numerous studies conducted on public perception point to a large gap between public opinion on the causes of homelessness and the actual causes of it. Agans et al. (2011) found that in public perception polls, drug and alcohol abuse continues to be ranked top on the list of probable causes of homelessness. This was followed by mental illness, lack of affordable housing, economic systems favoring the wealthy, a lack of government assistance, illness/handicaps, and irresponsible behavior. This public perception was fueled by the deinstitutionalization of individuals receiving mental health treatment under the Kennedy, Johnson, Nixon, and Reagan administrations (Baum & Burnes, 1993), as discussed earlier.

These perceptions do not accurately explain the current phenomenon of homelessness in the United States, however. In reality, based on the reasons articulated by those actually experiencing homelessness, the top causes of being without a home for families are, "(1) lack of affordable housing, (2) unemployment, (3) poverty, and (4) low wages." For individuals, "(1) lack of affordable housing, (2) unemployment, (3) poverty, (4) mental illness and the lack of needed services, and (5) substance abuse and the lack of needed services" top the list of reasons (National Law Center on Homelessness and Poverty, 2015, p. 3). Data repeatedly point to systemic factors as the leading causes of homelessness, indicating a wide gap between public perception and reality. This gap likely fuels some of the movements to criminalize homelessness and explains the general lack of public will to address it.

The Empathy Gap

Not surprisingly, the gap in perception leads to a lack of empathy among the general public for individuals experiencing homelessness. Gallop (2007) found that 85 percent of respondents from the general public listed drug and alcohol abuse as a major contributing factor to homelessness. This was followed by mental illness, post-traumatic stress disorder, and insufficient income at 67 percent, followed closely by job loss or unemployment. Lack of affordable housing was only mentioned by 48 percent.

People who rank drug and alcohol abuse as the top cause are statistically much less sympathetic to the issue (Agans et al., 2011). Those who rank a lack of access to affordable housing as the top cause are much more sympathetic. Race, level of education, and perceived seriousness of the issue all play into an individual's level of sympathy. Whites tend to be less sympathetic than nonwhites. As an individual's level of education increases, they also display less sympathy toward this issue. Additionally, if individuals view homelessness as a serious issue, they are more likely to be sympathetic. People rated as sympathetic also felt the issue was getting worse and that the role of the government was larger in assisting these individuals. Perhaps most interesting, this research found people with lived experience were "70% more sympathetic than those never having a homeless spell" (Agans et al., 2011, p. 5943). Nonwhites with a high school diploma or less who have lived experience are among the most sympathetic to this issue. Unfortunately, they are also the least likely to be heard on this issue.

However, by giving voice to those with lived experience, perhaps we can begin to bridge these gaps and understand the reality of homelessness. Only through building empathy will people begin to see this issue for what it really is and help to spark a national movement toward ending it.

One of the most troubling yet unsurprising aspects of our book is the realization that many of the contributors experiencing homelessness as adults had done everything right; some even came from middle-class families and had savings, a support network, and retirement plans. Many had good jobs and nice homes and were the picture of what most Americans view as successful. Yet, they lost everything due to a series of circumstances outside their control, eventually finding themselves without a place to live. It could happen to any one of us. In fact, it does. Redefining the narrative of homelessness in this country is necessary to create a more empathetic understanding of this issue.

About the Book

Organization of the Book

A main purpose of this book is to give voice to persons with lived experience, a voice that is so often neglected in discussions of the issue, with the understanding that one of the important ways for the public to shift its thinking about homelessness is to see and hear stories about people who have been through it. A second purpose is to begin to identify those factors that are instrumental in helping people emerge from their homelessness. Therefore, the book is organized around the nine chapters that include a first-person narrative from each of our contributors. These stories include:

- an explanation of what led to the contributor's homelessness,
- an examination of what that experience was like,
- an identification of what helped them get through the experience, and
- an explication of what homelessness has meant to them.

In addition to the stories themselves, some of the contributors included implications relevant to their experience. We have amplified these implications to focus on what the stories mean about homelessness more generally and how better to address the issue.

The Contributors

Contributors to the book are both men and women, they come from a variety of ethnic backgrounds, they have experienced homelessness at different stages in life, and their catalysts for becoming unhoused vary extensively. These differences serve to remind us that the term *homelessness* has nuances and subtleties that we must recognize. There is not one homelessness narrative; there are literally hundreds of thousands, each one with a different twist. This heterogeneity is absolutely critical to understand, so that the differences can be part of any discussion on how to best end this tragedy. The old adage "one size fits all" simply does not apply here. The country needs lots of different sizes, lengths, widths, and depths in order to meet the needs of this heterogeneous population.

Each of the contributors was selected for inclusion for a very specific reason. Barb represents the trauma of childhood homelessness. Tim was a runaway youth who also experienced foster care. Marie was part of a couch-surfing family who spent time bouncing from one long-term motel to another. Tiffany experienced the failure of reasonable and appropriate out-of-home placements as a teenager. Blizzard's situation was the result of a negative foster care experience. Leanne, a veteran, was the victim of a severe economic downturn. Michelle, a black veteran, suffered from both racial bias and an administrative error, a not-uncommon occurrence. A family battle forced James into homelessness, where he received inadequate legal advice. Finally, Caroline's misdiagnosed physical illnesses absorbed her entire life savings and pushed her into homelessness.

Despite these varied immediate causes of homelessness, all of our contributors experienced similar factors that helped them get through homelessness to a greater or lesser degree, namely, important human connections. In some instances, the connections were individuals who cared, including family members or teachers. In other cases, it was one or another kind of support group that expanded the natural networks of support. In every case, a sense of community was vital. More than anything else, it was these human connections, social capital if you will, that provided the basis for emergence from homelessness. In some cases, social service systems played a role; in others, educational systems were important. However, at the most fundamental level, it was the human connection that was crucial.

As these contributors have emerged from their homelessness, most have moved into important employment situations. They are teaching, advocating for the homeless, working in other types of education-related fields, campaigning for changes in how we deal with homelessness, finishing their own education, and the like. What is of particular interest is that all of them are deeply and passionately interested in the issue of homelessness and are committed to trying to improve how we as a nation combat this scourge.

As contributors, some have chosen to publish their chapter under a pseudonym. We encouraged each of them to make this decision based on their own circumstances, level of comfort in sharing their story, and family dynamics. Some contributors had a powerful desire to publish under their own names, wanting their story told. Several opted to use a pseudonym, and specific identifying details have been removed from the story to protect their identity. We do not differentiate between the two, or indicate which stories are which.

In having initial conversations with both individuals who decided to participate and those who eventually decided not to, the level of shame, trauma, and emotional complexities associated with living without a home became increasingly clear. In fact, several people we spoke with and asked to contribute ultimately refused. This was generally due to complex family dynamics, the fact that they did not want to share this portion of their past for fear of what people might think, or that the trauma of living without a home was so overwhelming that they were not ready to have this in black and white for the world to read, even under a pseudonym.

Themes of This Book

The original intent of this book, and one overarching theme, was to hear from people who have had this experience and who are now permanently housed. The idea was for them to inform how we approach this issue, as they are the most qualified to do so. Additionally, as indicated in the stories, stability is a spectrum. In most of the contributors' cases, they are now living in a safe, stable home. However, a few of them tiptoe on the edge of remaining housed, as is often the case with those who have experienced homelessness. The contributors represent a wide range on the continuum of stability. In meeting and listening to many of the contributors, they indicated that this is one of their biggest fears, even if they are permanently housed—the knowledge of how quickly that can change. This idea, the fluidity of housing, is another underlying theme of this book. That fear and realization are both evident in speaking with these contributors and are present throughout their stories as they move in and out of being stably housed.

Another theme, and perhaps one of the most powerful ones uncovered as a result of hearing these stories, is the role individuals played in the majority of the contributors ultimately becoming housed. Many of them had that one person, or handful of people, who helped equip them with a path out of homelessness. For some, it was an educator, some a family friend, or even a staff member at one of the agencies working with them. Mostly, it was just one person who believed in them. In trying to articulate this concept, we originally dubbed it "empowerment." We tested that terminology with the contributors, and one of them put it best in describing one of her people. She said, "It's not that she 'empowered' me. She didn't give me power. I already had my own power. She gave me the tools." This anecdote helps further strengthen the importance of hearing directly from individuals with lived experience, as there is always a danger in researchers unknowingly misrepresenting or potentially misinterpreting these experiences, inadvertently relaying misinformation regarding a certain issue, in the process of writing about them. In the final chapter, we explore at length this idea of "equipping" individuals as a potential policy and programmatic concept for ending homelessness.

Sampling

This book is not a representative sample of all homelessness variations, nor should it be considered a carefully controlled scientific study. Rather, it is a convenience sampling comprised of people who have experienced life without a home and met one of the federal definitions of homelessness discussed earlier in this chapter. Their experiences took place in various parts of the United States, though many occurred in our home state of Colorado; they were the result of a variety of circumstances, and they span from childhood to adulthood. We became familiar with each one of the contributors through our work—Don through the Burnes Center and Jamie through her work on homelessness at the local and state levels through the Continuum of Care.

We acknowledge this book does not address every one of the factors or living situations that comprise homelessness. In fact, it would be nearly impossible to do so. There is not a contribution from someone who is struggling with mental illness or a direct substance abuse disorder, though in the case of childhood and youth homelessness, these types of stories are portrayed through the eyes of the children whose parents struggled with these challenges. These are two voices we specifically sought to include, but we found such individuals disinclined to participate, understandably so. For similar reasons, we also did not include an individual who experienced homelessness as a result of escaping domestic violence. Additionally, we were unable to address all living situations, such as deeply exploring life in shelters or other transitional living situations, though some of our contributors reference this experience in their stories. We also recognize a larger discussion is needed on the disproportionate number of the LGBTQ community that experience homelessness, perhaps most disturbingly among America's youth.

While there are underlying themes, it would take volumes to explore all types of homelessness, for all subpopulations, and for all the various reasons one might find oneself unhoused. We acknowledge this limitation of the book and encourage readers to recognize that this is a small, geographically limited, nonrepresentative sample of the total population of people without homes. These stories do not, and cannot, speak for everyone experiencing homelessness. Therefore, it would be dangerous and irresponsible to characterize the entire issue of homelessness as framed within these pages. Narrative storytelling also inherently has certain limitations such as issues with the recollection of the subject, biases, and the danger of the facts being "remembered facts" and not necessarily historical truths (Polkinghorne, 2007). However, this book does provide unique and valuable insights into the experience through first-person explorations, and we do explore at length the factors that have helped our contributors move beyond homelessness. It is intended to provide readers with a more robust understanding of who might find themselves without a home and the reasons for it, as well as to combat the commonly held stereotypes on the issue that fuel misguided policy and practice.

The Stories

The stories in this book are raw. While some of the contributors have had experience and coaching in how to articulate their story and some stories are more refined than others, these are not professional writers, nor did we seek to deeply edit any of the stories. Due to the nature of the subject, there are instances of strong language and disturbing content, but the personality and message of each contributor has been preserved to ensure the story is truly his or her own. Each contributor has a unique voice, leading to some chapters that may create strong reactions. We feel this individual flavor adds significantly to the authenticity of the book. It can be messy in places, but so is the topic itself.

The chapters are organized generally in chronological order by the age at which the experience occurred, starting with child and family homelessness. It seemed the only natural way to organize the stories while providing some sort of consistent flow and continuity.

The Conclusion

In the concluding chapter, we focus on two topics. First, we summarize briefly the major points that our contributors have raised in their various stories. Then we explore in more detail some of the important implications that have surfaced and what these may mean for creating new and diverse ways to address homelessness. Although there are some encouraging signs regarding how we are currently providing housing and services, the truth of the matter is that we seem to be managing the problem, but we are far from solving it. It is our fervent hope that through these brave voices of lived experience and the lessons that can be drawn from them, we may develop new ideas and strategies that will improve our ability to address this crisis.

Notes

1. See, for example, Baumohl, 1996; Blau, 1992; Desmond, 2016; Gladwell, 2006; Gowan, 2010; Hoch and Slayton, 1990; Jencks, 1994; Kozol, 1987; Kusmer, 2002; Liebow, 1993; Miller, 1991; Rollinson & Pardeck, 2006; Snow and Anderson, 1993; Williams, 2003; Wilson, 1987; Wright, 1989.

2. There are numerous examples of quantitative and epidemiological studies of homelessness. Ellen Bassuk, Martha Burt, Dennis Culhane, Jill Khadduri, Deborah Padgett, Peter Rossi, Mary Beth Shinn, and Paul Toro, among others, have written extensively on homelessness. Also, federal departments and national organizations routinely put out annual statistics about the characteristics of homelessness. For a recent and thorough examination of various aspects of the issue, see various chapters in Burnes & DiLeo, 2016.

3. It is interesting to note that, in scanning recent bibliographies of writing and research on homelessness, many of the citations are from before the turn of the twenty-first century. Despite recent advances in our understanding of homelessness and its many facets, we still rely on a literature that precedes much of the more nuanced and sophisticated enlightenment about the issue and those who are the victims of it.

2

A Caring Adult: Barb's Journey

Barb's story is about a young girl who became emotionally homeless at the age of four and literally homeless for six years, starting at the age of six. Abandoned by an alcoholic father and stepmother, she roamed the streets of her small town, hiding out with her younger brother in nooks and crannies and in a beat-up old car. Her indomitable spirit, fueled by her young faith and her attachment to school and to her teachers, enabled her to reconnect with her biological mother and begin a stunning trajectory of success. Her story demonstrates the importance of hope, caring adults, and the potential safe place that school can be for children experiencing homelessness. It also provides an interesting juxtaposition of having a place to live versus having a *home*.

Barb's Story

Having a tough childhood and growing up in a dysfunctional family is nothing new for many Americans. In addition, alcoholism and poverty are often at the root of a downward spiral that leads to homelessness, as it was for me. But regardless of the circumstances that caused the less than ideal childhood conditions for these many individuals, I can tell you that all that starts badly doesn't necessarily have to end badly. The tremendous lessons learned that come from such a negative beginning, actually one day can become the blessing that gives your life meaning and purpose. I'm not suggesting there isn't a downside to poverty and homelessness, but rather than trying to totally focus on prevention of the conditions, it may be equally productive to focus on how to influence the perspectives and attitudes toward those conditions and circumstances such that it leads to an expectant outlook about life, regardless of the bleak surroundings. But for me, hopelessness was never a part of my homelessness experience. Don't get me wrong—I remember being absolutely terrified at times, not just frightened but terrified. There were many times when I did not know exactly where I would sleep, or how I would keep warm, or how I would eat. But regardless of these adverse conditions, I always knew I would have a better life.

Home

My experience of homelessness began long before my father lost physical possession of our house. Once everything you identify with representing "home" is gone, you are in essence homeless whether you have four physical walls surrounding you and a roof over your head or not. Home, more than anything else, is a mental or emotional construct. It is not just about a physical space.

In my case, the stability and sanctuary that I craved was at times a car, or a homemade fort in the woods, or a corner in the laundromat, or the alcove entry of a local grocery store. Each of these spaces conformed to the architecture of my heart and soul and provided what I needed most—sanctuary from a world of judgment, ridicule, and even repulsion, simply because I was poor, and dirty, and didn't fit in or meet the standards set by others. It takes much more than walls or rafters or bricks and mortar to protect you from these things.

From the ages of about six to twelve, I was eventually totally on my own for practical purposes. I fended for myself. I had parents—a father and a stepmother, but they were indisposed and unavailable. They were barely functioning alcoholics. Completely and totally unavailable. Thus, I grew up a "ragamuffin"—a term I am particularly fond of. A street urchin if you will. But it didn't start out that way. It happened over time.

Mom and Dad

Soon after my dad graduated from high school, he and my mother got married. My mother was only sixteen. She never finished school. Less than nine months later my first brother was born. Then another son, and then another son, and then me. I was my mom and dad's last child, and the only girl. I really don't know how my parents' relationship was back then—I was less than a year old. But I do know how their relationship ended. I know that booze played a big part in the eventual demise of my parents' marriage. The only thing I know for sure is that within a year of my brother's tragic death in a house fire and my birth, my father found refuge in alcohol—for the rest of his life. As for my mother, she was a teetotaler and never drank, so instead, she ran off with another man—on a motorcycle, headed to Florida. She left behind her two remaining sons and her infant daughter. But she would be back and do her best to rescue us.

The Aftermath

After Mom left, Dad and my grandfather asked my aunt, my father's sister, if she would take care of me, seeing that my grandmother was not able to. My aunt said yes, and I'm so very glad she did. She was the best thing that ever happened to me as a child. Her love and care provided me with the only home that I had ever known growing up. Living with my aunt was my first experience of feeling stable and normal. Her home was clean, the beds had sheets on them, and they were changed regularly. She was always cooking too. There were homemade cookies and cakes and regular sit-down meals. I felt warm; I felt safe; I felt secure. The stability that I found living with my aunt would not last very long. I was with her from age one to age four, and then everything changed in just one single night.

The Night That Changed My Life

I learned many years later that my aunt had made a promise to my father after my parents divorced. She agreed that she would take care of me until my father remarried, at which time she promised that she would "give me back" to him. It's a promise that I wish, and she wishes, she had never kept. When I was four, my father did remarry. He married a woman who was a waitress in one of the bars that he frequented. Being four, I didn't really understand the concept of marriage, and I certainly had no knowledge or understanding of the agreement that my father and aunt had made regarding who would "get me" once my father remarried and how much that would influence the rest of my life. This is how I remember leaving the only home I had ever known and moving to my father's house.

My father came into my aunt's house one night, and he and my aunt got into a terrible fight. There was a lot of yelling and then I heard a door slam. The next thing I know my aunt came into the room where I slept, seeming very upset—I had never seen her upset before. She instructed me to gather up my things and guided me down the stairs to the front door. She took me out on the porch. I remember that it was almost dark, cold, with a light drizzle coming down. She pointed around the corner and directed me to "go down there to your father's house." I could see the lights of another house, but that house seemed like a long way away. I was confused and had no idea what was happening. I had never walked that far by myself before. In reality, the house was not that far viewed through adult eyes—probably only 120 yards or so. But to a four-year-old, it might as well have been to the end of the world. That's what it seemed like to me. My aunt's voice was quite stern, and I wanted to obey her and do what she asked. It was pretty dark, and the road was wet. I remember walking very slowly, being very cautious with my steps because I had no idea where I was going exactly. When I got closer, I could see the light on the front porch, and I stepped up to the door and knocked. A woman that I had never met before answered the door. It was my stepmother. When she answered the door I just stood there—I didn't say a word, but she did. She looked at me and said, "What are you doing here? We don't want you." And then she closed the door.

Being confused and truly just lost, I turned around and went back to the road. Not knowing what to do or which way to go, I just stood there—absolutely frozen in fear, and totally terrified. I closed my eyes as tightly as I could—really, really tight—and that Sunday school song came into my mind—He's got the whole world in his hands, he's got the little bitty baby in his hands—that I sang when I played alone in my aunt's sewing room. In the next moment, with my eyes still closed, I heard a voice, God's voice. And that voice asked this terrified, lost little girl, "Do you want to live or do you want to die?" And in a whimpering little voice I responded, "I want to live." And the voice said, "Then you hang onto my hand and don't you ever let go." And I reached up, eyes still closed, and I grabbed on— the hand was large, and I could only manage to grab onto a thumb, but I never let go. My life changed that night forever. To this day, I have no idea how I got out of the street or what happened next. What I can tell you is that my next memory is at age six when I was getting on the school bus for the first time in front of my father's house, standing in the exact same place where I had the encounter with my blessed Savior.

Shortly after I started kindergarten, my father and stepmother moved into the small town where my grandfather first owned a boarding house. My dad and stepmother also had a child together, a little boy we called Junior who would soon become my daily shadow, following me everywhere—because I became his everything. That's what happens when you have nobody else around to take care of you. We were quite a pair of ragamuffins.

Losing the House

The last straw for my father was when he lost the house. He was clearly unhappy, depressed, and an alcoholic before then. But losing the house was the end for him. He never recovered from that loss, and he never tried. While still in the house, I watched my father give up. He quit his good job with the county. He and my stepmother, who was also a severe alcoholic, had knock-down, drag-out fights almost daily. The yelling and the screaming were intolerable. I spent almost all my time wandering the streets, even before we lost the house. My brother Junior and I ended up squatters in our own home. The very place that my father had remodeled and was so proud of became a filthy, disgusting hellhole. Garbage and trash would be crammed into the closets to the point where you couldn't get inside them. Filthy, dirty clothes were piled in every room. There was no food in the refrigerator ever. The electricity had been turned off due to delinquent bills not being paid. The house was cold. We would turn on flash lights to have some light at night. Junior and I would sleep on top of some of those dirty clothes on the floor, or in two chairs facing each other in the living room because it was just too cold or filled with garbage upstairs.

With the electricity and water cut off, and now, no source of heat, it became more and more difficult to live in that structure. My dad returned to the bar, and we saw less and less of him or my stepmother. Junior and I started sleeping at the laundromat because it was open twenty-four hours and it was always warm in there. Sometimes I would even scrounge up a dime or two by returning pop bottles for deposit just so I could run the dryers in the middle of the night, so we would have more heat. Eventually it became official. The financial institution who loaned my father money to remodel foreclosed on the house because he was in arrears about $750.

Finding Refuge

It was living with my aunt that I was first introduced to the notion that cars were a safe, secure place out of a storm. Interestingly, the notion that a car is a very safe place to be has never left me. The car became my go-to place for refuge, not only as a toddler in the arms of my aunt, but also as a homeless twelve-year-old, and even as a thirty-five-year-old grown adult seeking refuge from a storm of a different kind. That's when I rediscovered how much comfort a car could bring—how secure and safe you can feel when you lock the doors, muffle the sound of the streets, and scoot down in the back where no one could see you, away from intruding neighbors, uninvited firemen, and bill collectors. You could build quite a little hideaway in a car.

My automobile refuge as a child was a station wagon, with lots of room in the back, and I loved it. I created a whole fort in there. I had little cubbyholes with candy I had gathered at Halloween and places to store pairs of socks or other items that I found left in the washers and dryers at the laundromat. I had books to read, and a battery-powered lantern that I confiscated from somewhere. I had old winter coats and other items that I stacked to make a comfortable bed. And it's where I would go to daydream about a better life and a better future. It's where I hid out away from all the chaotic and frightening circumstances surrounding me.

Having a hideout is pretty important when you don't want anyone to know about your situation. You see, the fact that I didn't have anyone to take care of me, and that I had been abandoned, and that we had lost our home, wasn't about my father. In my mind, it was about me. *My deep, deep shame, and need for hiding, didn't stem from the failings of my father. My deep, deep shame came from the fact that I was unworthy. I was a "nothing and a nobody" and didn't deserve to be cared for. I had to hide out so no one else would find that out.* My unworthiness would remain hidden and a secret.

That whole town became my stomping grounds. I knew every nook and cranny, and it supported me and provided the trinkets and tools and scraps of necessities that I needed to exist. It sustained me, and it's what allowed me to endure.

For the last couple of years that I was with my dad, I began to have the same daydream over and over while hiding out in that car. Being certain that I was a nothing and a nobody, I daydreamed about becoming somebody—someday. On some days, I would have this daydream with tears streaming down my face after being mocked by someone for having dirty clothes or after the school nurse hauled me out of the classroom for having head lice or realizing that I didn't really have any place to go for dinner like the other kids. As a teenager and a young adult, I was driven to become somebody. Even though I didn't know what that meant exactly or what that looked like, I was driven to achieve—and achieve I did. And school eventually became my conduit for all my achievement.

Mom to the Rescue

At some point, my mother came back from Florida, and she filed for divorce from my father. My mother made a point to visit several times a year. It was usually the holidays when she would visit—Christmas and Easter are what I remember most. She'd always bring us new clothes, dress us up, and take us for an outing to the park or the lake for a picnic. She usually brought at least one toy for my brothers and me. As usual, I hid my shame even from my mother. Then, about the fourth grade, my father started letting me stay a couple weeks each summer with my mother at her house in Rochester, NY, where she lived then, about three hours away. He also let me visit her one Christmas.

Visiting my mother's house was always like an out-of-body experience. It didn't seem real. It was so foreign and frankly quite uncomfortable. It was such a different life. At the same time, those two summer visits and that one Christmas visit gave me a glimpse of a life that was stable, secure, and mostly free from drama. My stepfather did drink some, and he and my mom would argue, but nothing like I had experienced with my dad and stepmother.

However, unbeknownst to me, my mother had been building a case to seek custody once again. She had solicited the help of one of her old friends who happened to be my sixth-grade teacher. This teacher had been feeding reports to my mother that entire school year. In one of those reports my teacher told my mother that someone had reported that I had been seen out very late at night on Main Street and sleeping in the entry alcove of the local A&P Food Market. The teacher warned her that she had better do something to "save this girl" before it was too late.

The Last Day of Sixth Grade

After my dad lost the house, he somehow managed to rent a duplex on Main Street. I'm not sure what the lag time was between us being evicted from the house on Pigtail Ally and us moving into the duplex. I don't remember any of it, but by the end of the sixth grade, at age twelve, I decided that I did have an out and I needed to take it. So, on the last day of the sixth grade I went straight from school to a phone booth and I called my mother. I told her that I wanted to come live with her. It was a gut-wrenching decision and the hardest one of my life. She told me that she had been waiting for that call and to stay right there at that phone booth until she could get there. I think I sat on the curb and sobbed into my hands for the entire three-hour wait. I never told my father I had called her or let him know of the decision I made. I didn't tell anyone. I just left. That night, sleeping in a bed with clean sheets, in Upstate New York, I cried myself to sleep, mostly thinking about Junior.

The next thing I knew, my mother had petitioned the courts for custody of me. I really didn't want to leave my dad, I just wanted things to get better—to be better. A date had been set for a hearing and my father had been summoned to appear. I was so looking forward to seeing my dad. I missed him. Even though he wasn't around much, he was still my dad. My brothers and I waited and waited for him to arrive at the courthouse. But he never showed up. I couldn't believe that he didn't come and fight for me.

School as a Haven

School had always been my refuge and my sanctuary. I loved school. It provided structure and stability for me. I never missed a day. In grade school, I was a very good student, well behaved and always anxious to learn and do well so my teachers would be proud of me. School became my sanctuary and teachers became my saving grace. In high school, I graduated as a junior by petitioning the New York State Board of Education to let me take the senior-year Regents Exams (the required tests to get course credit) during the summer break between my junior and senior years. It was a teacher who helped me arrange for this and fought to get me permission to try. Because of her, the board allowed me to take the senior exams, and I passed them all. I was given credit for a senior year that I had not even participated in, and I received my Regents diploma a year ahead of schedule. I'll never forget that teacher and her fighting spirit. She was such an inspiration to me.

I graduated from college with my undergraduate degree in three years. About eighteen years later, after working as a professional in the design and construction fields and starting my own design-build firm, my son was a freshman in college and my daughter was in her senior year of high school. I shut down my company, sold all of the assets, moved halfway across the country from New York to Colorado, and went back to school to complete my master's and PhD in two-and-a-half years. This eventually led to where I am today—the director of a university program in real estate and construction management, a position that some people might think represents being a "somebody." But for me, somewhere along the way, with God's help, I came to realize that being a somebody has nothing to do with where you come from, who your parents are, what your position is, what your circumstances might be, or your economic status. Everybody is a somebody and no one is a nobody. And making sure that every human being I encounter knows that has become my life's mission.

Shame, and Dignity Restored

The real tragedy in losing your house is that it makes all of the shameful conditions of your life visible for all to see. Your job-lessness, or your family's dysfunction, or your financial troubles, or your alcohol abuse, or your depression, or your drug addiction, or your mental instabilities, or whatever defects exist in your self-worth—they all get exposed when you lose your house. Our unworthiness is suddenly no longer hidden, and our true homelessness is revealed. Even losing a job due to no fault of our own, like a layoff, makes us feel ashamed—like we should have been able to do something to prevent it and we failed. Many of these societal trappings of acceptability—like having a job, or being able to pay your bills, or having a house, or having a spouse, or having kids, or having friends, or having whatever—are at the root of so much of our shame. It's unfortunate, but it's real. There's so much out there to make us feel bad when in truth, none of these things have anything to do with your worth or your value. Yet they rob us of our dignity when they are missing, or we lose them. As a child, as long as I could hide out, everything would be okay because the rest of the world wouldn't know about all of my family's human deficiencies. Only I would know. But once they become exposed, then the shame of it all is fully on display. That's when the deep, deep pain becomes most acute. It's a pain that can physically make your heart hurt. I believe that the issue of shame and restored dignity has been mostly over-looked when dealing with the homeless. It's why I think that most attempts to remedy the problem have fallen short.

Can you be "homeless" while still having a house to live in? The answer is yes. My homelessness story began long before my father actually lost physical possession of his house. But I do think that this perspective may help us begin to look for solutions that go beyond just providing physical shelter.

Implications

Need for a Safe, Stable Home

In this chapter, Barb found refuge in various places, such as cars, laundromats, and stores, due to the fact that her "home" was in such a state of disrepair and her family dysfunction was so great due to her father's grief and alcoholism. In fact, as subsequent chapters will suggest, each of the contributors was seeking a safe, stable place to live, and many of them specifically mentioned it when crafting their original implications.

Barb suggests her own implications as follows:

> The reason that I believe that we have not actually improved the homelessness situation in the United States very much is because too many people identify "home" as being a physical structure with four walls and a roof and miss the point of *home* altogether. This description identifies a "house," but it isn't what makes a home. For me, homelessness is the emotional state of not feeling safe, protected, cared for, or secure. It's the emotional state of feeling desperate, with no place to go, and no one to turn to. It's that emotional state of being alone and on your own. So, if this is the case, then it would only make sense that restoring these elements to your human existence would be a major step to ending homelessness.
>
> There's a reason that some people return to their tin and cardboard shack under the bridge, or their abandoned car, or their cubbyhole in an abandoned building after they have been provided a "perfectly good apartment" or some other form of residence. But instead, what that housing unit represents is just one more way that they don't measure up. What we are communicating is that their solution, which very well may be providing them shelter, warmth, comfort, and protection, is not good enough, and, therefore, they are not good enough. So, once again, their dignity has been stolen by our societal expectations and standards. The human spirit takes yet another hit, and these individuals move further and further from finding their way back home. I know it's hard to believe that a tin shack or an abandoned car could ever provide more comfort than a decent apartment with modest furnishings, a refrigerator, and a stove. But I assure you, it can. Understanding this may open the door to a whole new set of solutions for addressing homelessness—solutions that focus on the restoration of dignity first, and the reestablishment of housing second.

Barb's homelessness only came to an end when she was able to escape from her father's house and enter her mother's *home*. However, one of the aspects of homelessness evidenced in Barb's chapter is the level of lifelong trauma that living without a home can cause. As an adult, Barb still sought the refuge of an automobile in times of insecurity or instability. It was her safe place both as a child and into adulthood. In cases of such severe negative childhood experiences and neglect, it is important to adequately address them to prevent the negative outcomes associated in adulthood.

Addressing the Trauma of Childhood Homelessness

According to the American Psychological Association (2018), approximately half of school-aged children who experience homelessness suffer from anxiety and/or depression, and 20 percent of preschool children without a home have emotional issues so severe they require professional help. Yet, the poverty that generally accompanies homelessness means they are significantly less likely to access the care they need. These students are also twice as likely as their housed counterparts to be diagnosed with a learning disability, to be held back, and to receive disciplinary action such as suspension (American Psychological Association, Presidential Task Force on Psychology's Contribution to End Homelessness, 2009).

While homelessness, or more specifically the uncertainty that accompanies it, could directly cause these issues, oftentimes it is actually the ancillary experiences that accompany childhood homelessness that leave lifelong scars, as we see in Barb's chapter. It is the violence in the home. It is the addiction of a parent. It is a divorce or separation of family. It might even be the abuse or neglect that might accompany such an experience, all of which Barb suffered throughout her childhood years. These experiences can have lasting negative effects and represent a large, growing body of evidence suggesting that childhood experiences can have a lasting impact on the physical and emotional health of a child, as well as fundamentally disrupting brain development.

Adverse Childhood Experiences

Adverse Childhood Experiences (ACEs) are those experiences encountered as children that affect an individual's development and long-term health. The Substance Abuse and Mental Health Services Administration (2018) identified eleven ACEs: (1) physical abuse;

(2) sexual abuse; (3) emotional abuse; (4) physical neglect; (5) emotional neglect; (6) intimate partner violence; (7) mother treated violently; (8) substance abuse within household; (9) household mental illness; (10) parental separation or divorce; (11) incarcerated household member.

There is a growing body of evidence that the brains of children with histories of abuse develop differently from those with no history of abuse. According to a study published by the *American Journal of Psychiatry* (Lutz et al., 2017), abuse affects a child at the cellular level, disrupting brain function and connectivity, essentially decreasing white matter throughout the brain. The amount of white matter present in the brain impairs a child's ability to learn and process information. Additionally, the researchers found other alterations in the brains of abused children that led to impairments in their ability to regulate an array of cognitive processes, including emotion and attention. They concluded that this early abuse may cause lasting disruptions in the brain.

In 1995, the first large-scale study took place to measure the effects of ACEs on adults, which included over 17,000 participants (Felitti et al., 1998). This comprehensive look showed that adults with four or more ACEs were twice as likely to battle cancer than those with zero ACEs. Emotionally, these same individuals with four or more ACEs were 460 times more likely to struggle with depression. For those with six or more ACEs, their expected life span was twenty years less than those who had no ACEs during childhood (Jackson Nakazawa, 2015). This study was groundbreaking in establishing the ties between abuse and neglect as a child and the physical and emotional outcomes as adults.

Additionally, according to a study done by Seattle University, as the number of ACEs increases, so does the likelihood of adult homelessness (Sekharan, 2016). The study found that adults with no ACEs only had a 1.3 percent chance of experiencing homelessness. Conversely, those with eight ACEs experience homelessness at a rate of 33.3 percent.

The work on ACEs highlights the need to assist families with young children that are experiencing homelessness. HUD has historically emphasized the need to address chronic homelessness (i.e., those single adults with extensive histories of homelessness and with one or more disabilities). It is only very recently that HUD has acknowledged an equal need to focus attention on families with children. This is a major step forward in our effort to end homelessness, although we clearly need substantially greater resources.

The Role of One Caring Adult

In this chapter, and in subsequent ones, particularly those addressing child and youth homelessness, the contributor identifies one or even a few caring adults who make an impact. In Barb's case, she points to a teacher who helped alert her mother to the gravity of her situation, assisting her in building a case to seek custody. She also mentions another teacher who believed in her, advocating so that she might graduate early and pursue a post-secondary education that eventually resulted in the successful completion of a PhD. While her mother ultimately gave Barb a stable home, these two individuals were critical in her long-term success, suggesting that a caring adult can be crucial.

Thankfully, the field of child psychology has noticed the positive outcomes of a caring adult, which has led to the expansion of programs that offer youth access to these types of individuals, commonly found in mentoring programs. A successful mentor experience can lead to several positive outcomes, including "increases in their self-worth, perceived social acceptance, perceived scholastic competence, parental relationship quality, school value, and decreases in both drug and alcohol use" (Grossman & Rhodes, 2002, p. 208). However, this relationship cannot be taken lightly—a mentoring relationship terminated early has also been shown to have detrimental effects on a student's outcomes, the same as listed above. That being said, and as subsequent chapters indicate, just one caring adult in the life of a child or youth, or even an adult, can lead to significant positive outcomes and is critical in the fight to end homelessness.

3

Family-Centered Support:
Tim's Journey

As a teenager and a good student, Tim was confronted by a dysfunctional and tension-filled household. After the last straw, Tim managed to escape to a welcoming family headed by a favorite teacher and then to a happy foster family, both of which enabled him to grow and move forward. His story provides a glimpse into some of the reasons that teenagers leave home and become homeless, and it reinforces the importance of caring adults and the value of family-centered supports.

Tim's Story

My father and mother met on the West Coast and fell in love immediately. They were married within a few weeks, and she moved to the mountains to start a new life with him. She desperately wanted a loving partner, and her parents wanted her to find a good husband. She loved him dearly, and he started off as a good partner, but over time he became harsh with her. He became a heavy drinker along with many of his peers from work. He would party late into the night and sometimes not come home for a few days. Meanwhile, my mother became pregnant

---

with my older sister. My father knew enough about himself—he wasn't ready to parent—to ask my mother to have an abortion (still illegal) or give the child up for adoption. She knew she wanted to be a parent and threatened to leave him. He relented, and she delivered a healthy daughter. About five months later, she was pregnant with me and went through the same "negotiation" to keep me too. Not exactly the best conditions to start a family, but it was the best my mother could figure out.

They tried their best to raise two children, but my father would periodically get violent, typically after bouts of drinking. By the time I was seven years old, my mother had enough, enough of his neglect and enough of his belligerence and physical abuse. She decided to take the bold action of divorce, and after a year, she decided to move somewhere warmer with my sister and me, somewhere she could start over and perhaps survive on the measly $300 per month child support settlement she received thanks to a state legal system that discriminated against women in divorce proceedings. She moved to a southwestern state to start over as a single mother with two children.

Fast-forward to seventh grade. I was tired of the warm weather and wanted to go back to the mountains to ski. I also yearned for a relationship with my father, having only seen him a few times over the years. My mother told me that my father was still "sick" and that I'd be taking on a big challenge in living with him. But hey, I was eleven and thought I could handle anything. My sister joined me for the summer and the first few weeks of school, but she pulled the "ripcord" and went back to live with our mother after a few violent episodes we both witnessed between my father and his then-girlfriend.

I don't know why I stayed, and I think that neither my sister nor I really shared with our mom precisely what had happened. Although I knew I would miss my sister and my mom, I was determined to get back on the snow to bring back fond memories and nearly forgotten sensations of gliding down a ski hill. I learned to avoid my father whenever he was drunk, and by the end of the school year, I was experimenting with marijuana and alcohol too. Following in my father's footsteps, I would sometimes not make it home after hanging out late with other kids who weren't being "parented" all that much either.

The main thing my father wanted was for me to have a job. This served me just fine as I wanted money to fuel my favorite adrenaline sports—skiing in the winter and dirt motorcycling in the summer. Participating in these sports kept me hopeful for the future as both of them felt very liberating and they forced me to be in the moment, lest my attention wander and I crash. Looking back on those times I wonder if being in control of the rush of adrenaline was part of my mental therapy in coping with the ever-present fear of my father becoming violent. I worked all sorts of odd jobs including lawn mowing, snow shoveling, dishwashing and kitchen cleaning in restaurants, fixing snowmobiles, being a ski instructor, and working for my father on a variety of his piecemeal projects. We lived about ten miles from town, and the closest bus stop was over a mile away, so I walked and hitchhiked a lot until I got my driver's license.

As I entered high school, I discovered the auto shop program and enrolled in an elective called Consumer Auto. It was really exciting to me, as I had always been interested in exactly how things work, and I enjoyed how patient the teacher was with me and all the other students. I developed a great admiration for the teacher, and he recommended that I take some of the more advanced classes, which I did. I also ended up developing a great relationship with him. In taking these vocational automotive classes I made my father happy, as he was pleased that I was able to fix more things around the ranch. I also learned skills that I knew would be needed for me to follow one of my dreams of building a "fast car" from parts scavenged at the impound lot or the dump.

My father had a longtime girlfriend who worked as a waitress and struggled with her own alcoholism. Periodically, they both would drink and argue about things, and my father would get verbally abusive and sometimes physically violent with her. I was now getting to the age where I knew I needed to do something to stop this behavior, so I would try to intervene in order to de-escalate the situations, with limited success.

Sometime around the middle of December that year, domestic violence between my father and his girlfriend happened yet again, and I got into the middle of their argument. This time my intervention didn't work, and my father hit me and threw me into a wall. I recall screaming at him and then retreating to my bedroom, where I closed the door (it didn't lock), pulled out my shotgun, and loaded it up. My father calmed down and approached my bedroom door with an apology or two, but I was pretty clear with him that I was going to shoot if he came in. He decided to let me be. I think I stayed in there and cried myself to sleep, but I can't recall for certain. That was the evening when I realized I just couldn't live there anymore.

The next day at school, I asked my auto shop teacher for help, and he said "no problem" and didn't probe too deeply about the specifics. In fact, he took me in that evening. He and his wife (she was also a schoolteacher) welcomed me into their house right at the start of the winter break, which seemed amazing to me as they also had a young baby to care for. I couldn't believe it, but it was quite cathartic to have a couch to crash on and not be worried directly about my safety. My auto shop teacher and friend let my father know I was staying with him for a little bit. He and I actually had a great time cruising around and working on various mechanical projects together, which helped me keep my mind at ease and the time to pass quickly.

Escaping my violent home just took one visit to my friend and mentor, my auto shop teacher, whom I trusted and who had helped me before. But it was the hardest ask I've ever made. I had so many emotions running around in my head. I was simultaneously ashamed, scared, shy, suicidal, and thinking violent thoughts about my father. I knew that if I didn't ask for help, I would be on a downward spiral, and I had higher hopes for my future than that.

As I reflect on this "couch-surfing" experience, I remember feeling nearly every emotion one could imagine: fear, anger, uncertainty, self-doubt, low self-esteem, euphoria, hopelessness, and more. There was fear of what might happen if I couldn't continue to find a couch to sleep on, a place to shower, or food to eat. There was uncertainty about the future and the apparent loss of control about my own destiny. I felt hopeless about my ability to respond to the situation, and I had an unhealthy but necessary focus on what was wrong at the present time versus hope and dreaming of a brighter future.

I wasn't sleeping well, and my brain was continually racing. I remember reading anything I could get my hands on (e.g., *Reader's Digest, Popular Mechanics*, library books, etc.) to help me not have negative thoughts. Whenever I was with my teacher and his family, I made it a point to try and connect with them and not be distracted by my feelings, which was difficult. They really helped me by bringing me into their life without probing questions, judgment, or conditions of my staying with them.

After settling in for a few weeks or so on the couch of my friend and mentor, it was time to take action. My auto shop teacher helped arrange for some family counseling for my father, his girlfriend, and me. After a few sessions, we were able to agree that I needed a more stable family situation for a while. We agreed on finding a foster family that would satisfy my and my father's criteria. We ultimately ended in agreement on a family that my auto shop teacher found for us. My father agreed to pay $150 per month to cover my room and board, and I agreed to take on a high school sport (the foster family's only condition for my staying with them).

My foster family had raised two adult boys and had another son one year behind me in high school. The family was amazing, a great combination of discipline, respect, and love. I lived with them for about a year while I continued to attend high school and family counseling with my father and his girlfriend. Again, I felt incredibly lucky to be a part of this new family. The father was a paraplegic air force veteran who had served our country as a decorated bombardier, navigator, and radar observer, this after being one of 6,000 Japanese Americans in California who were "voluntary evacuees" and moved to the interior of the United States before the 1942 deadline. The mother was always available and supportive even when I made mistakes. Their youngest son and I became fast friends. In reflecting with him on his perceptions of that time when we were "stepbrothers," he said that he thought I had the "world wired" at that time. Even though I had plenty of self-doubt on the inside, my can-do attitude persevered, and I bounced back rather quickly. I started applying myself in school for the first time and realized that I could actually be a good student if I did homework—having a stable home situation really made a difference pretty quickly.

One of the highlights of my experience in living with a foster family was when my auto shop teacher encouraged me to enter a vocational skills contest—I won first place in automotive technology for the entire state. Apparently, this was a rare accomplishment for a junior in high school, but I had been fixing things and working as a mechanic since I was twelve or so. Part of the prize was a free trip to Kentucky for the Vocational

Skill Olympics and my first plane ride. I remember being awed by the president of the United States, who visited to court the coalition of unions that supported the event, and who spoke about the future need for technical workers. Not only was I pleased that I had bounced back from such a low point, but also that I had done so to honor both my auto shop teacher and my foster family. In fact, I remember saying to my foster family that I had dreams of someday becoming the CEO of General Motors and that I would buy them a Cadillac once I did. They really showed me how a strong family can overcome adversity (i.e., a paraplegic father who survived racism and a horrific plane crash, who worked hard with his caring wife to raise a family of three sons and one daughter) and still give back by helping someone like me whom they barely knew.

I have enduring relationships with and respect for those who helped me through that challenging time. Likely due to this experience, I have a deep commitment to the community and am dedicated to supporting others through their challenges. Thus, after graduating from school, it was easy for me to decide to move back to my hometown to pay it forward and give back to the same community that invested in me. In fact, my career is currently focused on social justice and creating systemic change for working-class immigrants in my community.

Thinking back on that period of my life, I can now articulate what home means to me: it's a warm and cozy place where I can be myself, relax from the stresses of the world, and enjoy the company of friends and family. It is a place where violence doesn't exist and where everyone feels safe. Living with my auto shop teacher, unlike living with my father and his girlfriend, created a warm and cozy place where I could be myself, relax, and be with friends. My teacher and his family became my family for a short time and then helped me find a warm and welcome foster family for over a year, while I worked through issues of my own and with my father.

I still have self-doubt that periodically emerges and makes me question my self-confidence. This tended to emerge most when I was in college. I would often convince myself that I was going to fail every test and never graduate. It wasn't until I was a junior in college that I realized that I was actually doing quite well and was on track to graduate with honors. On the positive side, I developed tenacity and resiliency about my ability to endure all sorts of challenges. I don't give up easily, and I still remind myself that if my upwardly mobile career as a middle-class manager stumbles, I have a fallback, namely, I can always work as an automotive mechanic—thanks in part to the relationships and skills I developed during that challenging time.

When I recently spoke to my auto shop teacher and his now ex-wife and thanked them for "saving my life," they each said they didn't think of it that way. They each said they were glad to help and that they would do it again. To me, this highlights the strong values they both had around helping others and the benefits of living in a small-town rural community. There were sufficient resources in the community and within their network for a workable solution to succeed without the need for formal policies or programs.

Replicating this kind of one-on-one support system in today's more networked world is perhaps more challenging. Today's social media networks seem to be larger in number but smaller in depth (e.g., thousands of friends on Facebook but fewer "close friends" that actually know you). Yet to me it is unclear if having a large online network would actually help in the case of an individual being homeless and needing just one key person to make a difference. I suspect that a person-to-person ask for help is what really needs to happen, not a plea for help on social media. When I hear about teen suicides, I often ponder the role that social media played both in identifying someone who needed help from others in his or her network and how that online network didn't respond with sufficient support to stave off the suicide.

Implications

Runaway and Throwaway Youth Experiencing Homelessness

Like so many other youths in his age group, Tim decided that he could no longer live at home with dysfunctional parents. After confronting his father in one of his father's fits of rage, Tim became a victim of his father's violence. The next morning, he joined the ranks of the runaway youth cohort, although he always had a place to stay because he was couch surfing with a teacher and then with a foster family.

A recent US Interagency Council on Homelessness report indicated that "almost 41,000 unaccompanied youth were identified as experiencing unsheltered or sheltered homelessness in America, according to the PIT counts conducted in January 2017. . . . More than half (55%) were unsheltered"; nearly half of these youth were white, and 34 percent were African American (2018c, p. 1). In a 2016 brief entitled "Homeless and Runaway Youth," the National Conference of State Legislatures indicated that "the National Runaway Switchboard estimates that on any given night there are approximately 1.3 million homeless youth. . . . It is estimated that 5,000 unaccompanied youth die every day as a result of assault, illness, or suicide" (p. 1). Although many of these youth will return home, many will not. An astounding 75 percent of runaways are female; up to 22 percent of the girls experiencing homelessness are pregnant; up to 40 percent identify as lesbian, gay, bisexual, transgender, or queer (LGBTQ); 46 percent report having been physically abused, 38 percent emotionally abused, and 17 percent forced into unwanted sexual activity by a family member; and 75 percent have dropped out or will drop out of school (National Conference of State Legislatures, 2016, p. 1). In fact, shame and/or uncertainty about sexual orientation or strong negative parental reaction to this causes many youth to leave home, thus accounting for the large percentages of homeless LGBTQ youth.

The brief goes on to say that the consequences of life on the street for these young people include increased likelihood of high-risk activity such as unprotected sex, having multiple sex partners, and illicit drug use; greater risk for depression and suicide; increased use of sex as a form of bartering for food, clothing, and shelter; and severe difficulty in school (National Conference of State Legislatures, 2016). For some, foster care is a revolving door until they reach the age of eighteen. For others, the streets, all-night shops, parks, and alleyways become home.

Tim was a lucky one; he had a teacher who was willing to take him in and act as go-between for him and his father. This caring teacher also made arrangements for a good foster care placement that helped Tim continue with his education. Many youth experiencing homelessness, unlike Tim, never have this type of support, leaving them to fend for themselves, potentially placing them in dangerous situations such as those discussed above.

A 2Gen Approach

For far too long, programs have focused on either the child or their caregivers separately, failing to recognize the link between the two. This type of focus leads to a fragmented approach at best, and an ineffective model at worst. For example, according to the task force report published by the American Psychological Association (2009), "Mothers who have not had the opportunity to heal from cumulative traumatic exposures often lack emotional resources needed to be positive role models or involved parents. Children living with depressed or traumatized parents are at risk for depression and behavioral dysfunction" (p. 22). Therefore, to end the cycles of poverty, trauma, and homelessness prevalent in our nation's children, a two-generation (2Gen) approach is necessary, working to meet the needs of both children and caregivers.

The 2Gen approach is multifaceted and includes connecting children to "high quality educational services" and parents to workforce development; assisting parents in gaining the "skills, knowledge, and resources to support their child's development"; establishing family access to "economic and social supports"; and assisting families in building the all-important social capital (Administration for Children and Families, n.d.).

Human services at the federal, state, and local levels have begun adopting this model in an effort to both streamline services, leading to more efficiency, and provide better outcomes for families and children. A study conducted by Ascend at the Aspen Institute found that the majority of Americans, regardless of political affiliation, support a two-generation approach even if it raised their income tax (Aspen Institute, 2014).

The 2Gen approach is gaining recognition in part due to its popularity on both sides of the political aisle but also due to its significant success when implemented correctly. This success is evidenced in multiple areas, such as "human services, education, labor and workforce, and health," to address several underlying issues related to homelessness, including "poverty, literacy, school readiness and family economic stability" (National Conference of State Legislatures, 2018). For example, a 2017 analysis of CAP Tulsa showed dramatic results when a quality Head Start program for children was paired with postsecondary health-care certification for their caregivers. A comparison group had a mere 3 percent certification obtainment rate, while those enrolled in the program demonstrated a 61 percent certification rate after just one year (Chase-Lansdale et al., 2017). Fiscally, this model also proves effective and responsible. An analysis conducted by Wilder Research (Diaz & Piña, 2013) of the Jeremiah Program, aimed at supporting single mothers and their children with affordable housing, access to high-quality early education, training in life skills and empowerment, coupled with education leading to a career, showed significant return on investment. For every private dollar invested in the Jeremiah Project, the analysis found an approximate return of $3.93 in benefits savings by decreasing the need for public assistance, generating increased taxable income, reducing crime, and shrinking the number of students requiring special education support.

From both a social and a fiscal perspective, a 2Gen approach is humane and responsible. It has bipartisan support and provides an effective model for addressing many of our society's underlying issues. While several states have adopted this approach, more legislative support is needed across the United States to create programs and models that address the whole family, ultimately breaking negative cycles of behavior.

Family Resource Centers

Tim provides some compelling implications around family dysfunction and how to support effective initiatives. He says, "While we cannot prevent unfit parents from producing offspring, there are ways to provide some assistance and resources to families that are struggling to deal with difficult issues in the home." One of the ways to provide a 2Gen approach is through family resource centers. In his implications, Tim's research describes the need for

> policies that promote and support funding for family resource centers in communities throughout the United States; this could make a big difference for homeless youth. . . . Family resource centers are local organizations in communities that families can turn to for support. . . . Their goal is simple: healthy families in healthy communities. They can provide safe, accessible places for families to access coordinated services to help them strengthen their families and become more self-reliant. Family resource centers have a rich history that grew out of the settlement house movements of the late 1800s, such as Hull House in Chicago founded by Jane Addams and Ellen G. Starr (Johnson, 2004), where immigrant families could find support. With its innovative social, educational, and artistic programs, Hull

House became the standard-bearer for the movement that had grown, by 1920, to almost 500 settlement houses nationally.

Tim went on to indicate that

family resource centers bring together services and activities that educate, develop skills, and promote positive family interactions to improve outcomes for both families and communities. This increases the capacity of families to be resilient, healthy, and involved members of their community. Services and activities at family resource centers are tailored to the demographics, culture, and needs of their local communities. This approach of involving families in problem solving while at the same time developing skills, abilities, and talents, works to invest in and support healthy and functioning families and communities (The California Family Resource Center Learning Circle, 2000).

Tim added,

According to James Garbarino in *Raising Children in a Socially Toxic Environment* (1995), the social context in which children grow up has become poisonous to their development. Garbarino suggests that there are a number of factors that can contribute to successful coping and resilience thereby reducing the impact of their toxic environment. Family resource centers are a great vehicle for communities to employ to help family members develop their skills to overcome these destructive factors. It is my belief that family resource centers can play a role in preventing situations like mine that if unaddressed can lead to youth becoming disenfranchised, hopeless, and subsequently homeless.

A central feature of these types of resources is the focus on the entire family as the arena for negotiation, understanding, and empowerment. In many cases, youth and their parents are brought together to build greater interpersonal strengths and cooperation. In reality the work of these centers is a precursor to the 2Gen approach.

The importance of a focus on the entire family is underscored by Rollinson and Pardeck (2006). They argued that the United States has never had a truly family-centered policy, and that recent federal programs, such as Temporary Assistance for Needy Families (TANF) and Supplemental Nutrition Assistance Program (SNAP), have further eroded the ability of families experiencing homelessness to deal with poverty and homelessness. They argued convincingly for a real family policy that provides for a decent standard of living for all children and families; provides for comprehensive health care for both children and adults; and includes comprehensive social services that meet the needs of the "modern family" (p. 86). The expansion of family resource centers would be an effective way to accomplish these goals.

Caring Adults and Networks of Support

As Tim has recounted, he was able to move successfully through a time in his life that could have been devastating. The keys to his positive transition were a caring teacher and a loving foster care family. As we will see throughout these stories, this human element is critical for a successful escape from living situations that could be truly disastrous. Caring adults and a positive, stable network of support proved invaluable for Tim, just as they did for our other contributors. Consequently, the need to create and facilitate the development of these two critical elements is a major theme throughout this book.

4

Expanded Housing Options: Marie's Journey

Marie's story highlights her housing instability, couch surfing, and life in long-term motels. It also describes a case in which Marie experienced homelessness according to the USED definition but not according to the HUD definition; this discrepancy leads to support under one system but not the other, something that disproportionately affects families with children. Marie's account describes the difficulty of finding a home when there is parental involvement in the criminal justice system. Further, it leads to an exploration of economic inequality and the failure of our system to produce adequate low-income housing, and it suggests the importance of school as a place for stability and for encouragement to pursue a college and postgraduate career.

Marie's Story

Family Background

Growing up, my family never seemed to have quite enough money to "make it." My father was an electrician by trade, and because he worked most of the time as an independent contractor, work was spotty. When there was a lot of work, my father made a good paycheck. When there was no work, our family struggled to get by. My mother was a school bus driver for the better part of her professional life and stopped working when I was born so that she could stay home and raise me. Because we were a family on a single income, money was always tight.

In addition to money just being tight, my parents had significant challenges in their lives that made it hard to maintain stable housing. At the time that we lost our housing, when I began high school—the most unstable housing situation of my life—both of my parents had formal evictions on their records, outstanding warrants for their arrests, and my mother struggled with, and still struggles with, substance use. Even though my mother and father both had warrants, they were for nonviolent crimes. My mother got into a car accident and when it came time for her to go to court, she had an anxiety attack and never appeared. Her failure to appear turned into a warrant for her arrest that she did not take care of because of her embarrassment at missing court due to a mental health issue and her inability to recognize that she needed to seek help for it. My father's warrant for his arrest stemmed from a disagreement with a former boss who claimed that he stole materials from a job site after my father quit his job. My father did not go to court because he could not afford a lawyer and did not know of the resources to find a lawyer to assist him for free.

Both of my parents were ashamed and unwilling to freely share that they had these challenges, and when it came time to apply for public assistance programs that could have helped them, they would miss meetings and not follow requirements. My parents were too embarrassed to share their barriers and thought they would make them ineligible for assistance, so they didn't ask for help. They did not have enough knowledge to navigate the system properly to meet these requirements, and if they would have had a caseworker tell them openly that they could assist in providing a referral to help them get their justice record cleared, things may have been different. Many programs assume that individuals in need of assistance will ask for help with whatever referral they may be in need of, whether it be with housing, mental health, or legal help, but do not consider that individuals are afraid of the stigma they may face and the shame they have, and they do not ask for the referral.

Housing Uncertainty and Doubled Up

The first place that my family landed after losing our housing the first time was with my aunt and uncle. We shared a room in the basement, and it was only for about a month until my parents found an apartment to live in. We were in the apartment for a couple of years when an opportunity opened up to live next door to my grandmother in a house that was purchased by my great-uncle. Years passed and led up to my freshman year of high school. My great-uncle had passed away, and my great-aunt decided to give our home to one of her handymen. We moved into another apartment, couldn't afford it, and then upon eviction from that apartment, we moved again.

My mother, my sister, and I moved in with my aunt, uncle, and cousin, forced to live separately from my father. My mother and my aunt argued and became frustrated with each other many times over the closeness of space, plans moving forward, and my mother and father's ability to continue to raise us children even though we were close to adulthood. My mother's mental health, depression, and alcoholism deteriorated the longer she stayed in my aunt's home, as she struggled to keep a grasp on her family and provide us with basic needs. When my aunt would try and step in and help, my mother felt like more of a burden, and in less shape to ask for help.

Life at my aunt and uncle's house was warm and inviting, but it never truly felt like home. Being doubled up in someone's home means that you must learn the way that the house is run, and if there was something that wasn't working, you really couldn't change it. As a teenager, I was independent. I was accustomed to leaving the house and taking the bus when I felt like it, never eating at the dinner table, and having a TV in my room. My aunt and uncle, the great people that they were, allowed my sister and me to have a TV, but they were really big on us coming out of our room and spending time downstairs with the family. This was something I had to become accustomed to.

The hardest part about being doubled up is that you are never sure how long the arrangement is going to last, and you hold on to it being temporary. What could have been seen as stability throughout my time in high school staying at my aunt's house was actually insecurity. Although I knew my aunt and uncle would never ask my sister and me to leave, it always felt imminent, and I was always waiting for my parents to move in somewhere we would go back to full-time.

About six months after my mother, my sister, and I moved into my aunt's home, my mother and father decided to move into a motel so that they could be together and see us on the weekends. When I wasn't at my aunt's house, I was at one of the motels where my parents were staying. Motel life was different than staying with family in their home. In a motel, there is usually one and possibly two rooms for the four of you to share. There is often no microwave, refrigerator, or any way to store your food, and sleeping consisted of my mom, my sister, and me on the bed while my dad had to take the floor. Because there is no microwave or fridge, no food is prepared, and you eat out for every meal. There is a TV to watch and that is really the only form of entertainment. The spaces were small, and I was always looking for an excuse to leave to hang out with friends. My mother and father were in and out of motels for about two and a half years. Some motel stays were longer than others, but the average stay per motel was usually a few months. Initially, we had a few motels in town that were farther from my school and in less desirable neighborhoods. I was always afraid that people would see me go into the motels and start talking.

Right before I graduated high school, my parents' situation changed, and they were able to move out of the motel where they were staying. My parents' situation changed because a friend that they met told them about an apartment that would look past rental history and criminal justice involvement. It was not due to any program but a friend who was willing to recognize their barriers and find a realistic solution for them. Now that I am an adult and work in the social services field, I know that they could have turned to agencies for help in finding an apartment that would help them look past this. It would be helpful for agencies to be upfront with individuals about what they can offer and what situations they will work with. My parents' overall distrust of agencies and lack of information as to what they could have offered likely extended their time without a home more than necessary.

I feel like it is important to share that in staying at my aunt's and staying in the motels, I was taken care of by family that cared deeply for me. Whether families are doubled up or staying in a shelter, car, or on the streets, there is an underlying assumption by our society that that family just doesn't care about their children. It is important for me as a child in that situation and as a professional who now works with families without a home each day, that we are making sure that we are not coming to that conclusion. A parent's primary job is to be a parent. A child who is experiencing homelessness does not necessarily have parents who do not care. In a way, families who are living doubled up or staying in a motel are trying their best to not have their children experience the traumatic homelessness industrial complex, which includes unsafe and unstable shelters. Families living doubled up and in motels are often trying to prevent homelessness without the help of social services and government agencies, as those agencies typically do not provide assistance to families in these types of living situations.

High School and College

In high school, I was introduced to a program in my school system that hired individuals as homeless liaisons for students experiencing homelessness to receive supportive services. The program (known at the time as the Education Outreach Program) came out of the McKinney-Vento Homelessness Act. At the time I was in school, the program was underdeveloped, and I met with someone once a month after school to receive a free bus pass for being labeled as "homeless."

Receiving the free bus pass each month quickly became of interest to my peers. I felt awkward for having to explain this situation, and that being disadvantaged at home got me something that nobody else was able to get. I also felt ashamed for not having to do any hours of work in the kitchen, and for simply getting a bus pass for something that was out of my control.

Many of my teachers did not know what my family situation was like at home. I was a high-performing student, well behaved, quiet, and did everything in school that was asked of me. I took Advanced Placement classes, never had any trouble turning in homework, worked a part-time job at Kmart, and for the most part, got by without being asked many questions at all about my home life.

The only teacher in my school who was tuned in to my home life situation was my Junior Reserve Officers' Training Corps (JROTC) instructor, who I referred to as Colonel. My JROTC instructor became a significant mentor for me over my time in school, and over the years that I stayed involved in JROTC, he took the time to get to know me even with my quiet and put-together personality. I grew to trust him as the adult that I would open up to in the building and share my story with. The JROTC class that I was in was unique in that it seemed like all of us were close to falling apart without the support of each other. Every single person in my class seemed to have some sort of hectic home life and struggle that they were going through. We confided in Colonel, and in each other, as supports that we trusted. I slowly opened up to Colonel about my life as the years passed in high school. I remember first telling him about how I lived with my aunt and uncle, which was not too uncommon for students in my high school. As time passed, I told him about how I was also living with my parents at a motel over the weekend.

What I appreciated most about Colonel was how he listened without judgment, and how he did not immediately try to interfere in the situation. I was always afraid of adults finding out about my hectic home life because I was always afraid that they would jump to the conclusion that it was an unsafe place to be in, and that I needed to get out of that situation as soon as possible. Colonel never put his opinion forward about my lifestyle, and instead, would just ask if there were supports that I needed. Most importantly, he trusted when I said I didn't need anything; he never pressed me on it. My JROTC class pushed the ideas that all of us had enormous potential. We were encouraged to capitalize on that potential both in high school and in the future. Ironically, for many of us, our potential did not mean joining the military, even after spending four years in JROTC. For many of us, that meant seeking out colleges that would best fit our needs. In my JROTC classes, we discussed going to college in a different way than what I heard in other classes. We discussed it not just as furthering studies, but as growing in a way that made sense to me. It was in these classes that I began to see college as a way to continue the one thing that was constant in my life—going to school.

My physical situation of being without a home changed because I was accepted into a university and decided to begin college there. For the first time in four years, I moved into a place where I felt grounded. I had control over my situation, and I was able to make my own decisions about when and where I would move in the years to come. In my junior year of college, I was accepted into a special postbaccalaureate program for achievement, which was designed to prepare underrepresented students for doctoral studies through research and preparation work for graduate school. Being part of this program meant that I would be attending graduate school right after my undergraduate studies finished up, and that I would not immediately move into teaching in a public school. Through some coaching with my instructors in this postbaccalaureate program, I realized that a more appropriate fit for what I wanted to do was social work. As I was finishing college, I was accepted to eleven graduate schools of social work across the country. I was faced with the choice of going Ivy League, going private, or going to another public university.

In the fall, I began school at a well-known graduate school of social work. It was in the field of social work that I truly began feeling as though my personal values were matched with those of my profession. I felt as though I could truly live out my personal values of service and social justice by working as a social worker. It was also in graduate school when I began to identify my adolescent experience of not having a steady home as one of "experiencing homelessness."

In graduate school, there was a focus on individual experience as a way to relate to clients and to the world, as well as relate to the major social problems of our day. In my graduate class, as well as I am sure many others across the country, homelessness comes up as a social condition that our society has not acted on. I don't think that many of us who have lived a life where they were without a home tend to identify themselves as being homeless. I think this is because of the term itself, homeless. As a society, we have been conditioned to imagine someone who is "homeless" to be standing on the street corner holding a sign or sleeping in the park. I never felt as though my situation was bad enough to claim that I was experiencing homelessness, and it felt (and still feels) disingenuous to do so. I am not saying that my experience in staying in motels and doubling up with family is not something that can be compared to living in one's car or sleeping on the sidewalk or staying in a shelter. It feels like in many ways that the experience I went through was one that was a light touch into what can often be a traumatic experience of living unsheltered. Because it is difficult to categorize what situations meet or feel like "homelessness," I feel like we should shift to a more inclusive term like "being without a home." Being without a home can encompass many stories of individuals and families that have not had a place to stay.

To me, having a home means having a place that is steady enough where you aren't worried about what stuff you are leaving behind each time you move. At the age of ten, I started becoming responsible for moving my own awards from school, family photos, and other mementos. I never knew what precious memory I might be leaving behind every time we moved. In fact, it wasn't until this year when I felt ready enough to give the family photo album back to my mother. Being without a home is also being without the ability to have control over physical space. When I was without a home during high school, I never knew when we were going to move to another motel room, or if I would need to leave the room in my aunt's home. I never felt grounded in any one place until I landed in my college dorm.

It has now been roughly seven and a half years since I made the decision to go to college, and I finally feel grounded. In that time, I have attained a bachelor's degree in social science: secondary teaching and a master's degree in social work, I have had the opportunity to practice social work around the world in Africa and Central America, and I have maintained a steady home for myself. Currently, I have the opportunity to serve families experiencing homelessness as a case manager. It is in doing this work where I truly feel at home, and where I get the opportunity to empower families to move through their housing crisis and rapidly get back into a home for them to settle into.

Implications

Caught in the In-Between

Much of the national discussion about homelessness only focuses on the individuals deemed "literally homeless"; it does not address the millions of Americans, many of whom are families with children, who meet the other definitions of homelessness, such as the USED definition, but do not qualify for housing assistance through HUD-funded programs. They are caught in the in-between. In Marie's story, her parents technically would not have qualified for housing assistance through these traditional housing programs, as her parents would not have been recognized as fitting the narrow HUD definition of homelessness.

As we indicated in Chapter 1, the differences between the HUD definition and the USED definition are nontrivial. According to the USED definition, there are over 1.3 million students enrolled in our public schools identified as experiencing homelessness, three-quarters of whom are living in doubled-up situations; these are families that are forced to live with relatives, friends, or even strangers, with no legal right to the home, in conditions that are often inadequate. The HUD definition acknowledges only one-fifth of that number. Furthermore, for every school-age child in a family experiencing homelessness, there is on average one additional child under the age of six not yet enrolled in school and thus not counted in the data (US Interagency Council on Homelessness, 2018b). This suggests that there may be as many as 2.6 million children under the age of eighteen experiencing homelessness by USED's definition, or ten times the number according to HUD.

There has been considerable debate about the existence of two very different definitions of homelessness being used by different federal departments. HUD's argument seems to be that a family that is doubled up does have a place to live, with the assumption that this doubling up situation can go on for an extended period of time. However, HUD also considers people in transitional housing, who can generally remain there for up to two years, homeless because at the end of two years, they are not assured of housing.

There is an interesting irony here; individuals and families with children who are living in temporary doubled-up situations are not generally considered homeless under the HUD definitions. On the other hand, individuals and families with children who are assured of their own housing in transitional facilities for up to 24 months are considered to be experiencing homelessness. USED recognizes that students in a doubled-up housing unit will, in all likelihood, have no separate space to do their homework, will be interrupted by other children and a number of adults, and could have trouble getting enough sleep, all of which will work to undermine the student's ability to do well in school. They also recognize that with no legal rights to the home, with an often tense living situation due to the strain this type of arrangement puts on all members of the household, and with the potential for a family to be asked to leave at any point with virtually no due process, these families can bounce from place to place. Therefore, the US Department of Education, through the McKinney-Vento legislation, provides services to students in a broader range of unstable housing situations to help ensure that at least the child's school remains a safe, stable constant. However, as we point out in Chapter 1, they will only receive housing assistance if they meet the HUD definition of homelessness. Marie's family was in exactly this predicament.

The definitional battle continues today: there is currently draft legislation in the House of Representatives to use only the USED definition for all federal agencies. How this will turn out is anyone's guess. However, we feel it is imperative that families that are doubled up should have direct and immediate access to housing assistance. There should be no in-between families or students.

Economic Inequality

The in-between nature of Marie's family's housing situation reminds us that in addition to those families without a home by HUD's definition there are millions of families that are in extreme poverty, some of whom are forced to double up and/or stay in motels, others of whom are on the cusp of becoming homeless. This level of poverty and homelessness is in stark contrast to those at the other end of the economic scale.

An indication of the inequities in our system can be summarized by a special report from the United Nations. Despite the claim by the Council of Economic Advisers that "the vast majority of Americans today are able to meet their basic needs" (2018, p. 24), Philip Alston (2018), the special rapporteur of the UN Human Rights Council, presented a very different picture:

But its [the US] immense wealth and expertise stand in shocking contrast with the conditions in which vast numbers of its citizens live. About 40 million live in poverty, 18.5 million in extreme poverty and 5.3 million live in Third World conditions of absolute poverty. It has the highest youth poverty rate. . . . Its citizens live shorter and sicker lives compared to those living in other rich democracies, eradicable tropical diseases are increasingly prevalent, and it has the world's highest incarceration rate, one of the lowest levels of voter registration among OECD countries and the highest obesity levels in the developed world. The United States has the highest rate of income inequality among Western countries. (p. 3)

Alston went on to quote a 2017 report from the International Monetary Fund, stating that the United States "is delivering better living standards for only a few" (p. 4) and that

household incomes are stagnating for a large share of the population, job opportunities are deteriorating, prospects for upward mobility are waning, and economic gains are increasingly accruing to those that are already wealthy. . . . The United States now has one of the lowest rates of intergenerational social mobility of any of the rich countries. Zip codes, which are usually reliable proxies for race and wealth, are radically reliable predictors of a child's future employment and income prospects. (pp. 4–5)

Later on, in a section entitled "Who Are the Poor?," Alston stated,

In thinking about poverty, it is striking how much weight is given to caricatured narratives about the purported differences between rich and poor that are consistently peddled by some politicians and media. The rich are industrious, entrepreneurial, patriotic and the drivers of economic success. The poor are wasters, losers, and scammers. As a result, money spent on welfare is money down the drain. . . . In imagining the poor, racist stereotypes are usually not far beneath the surface. . . . Similarly, large numbers of welfare recipients are assumed to be living high on "the dole." . . . But in reality, the poor are overwhelmingly those born into poverty, or those thrust there by circumstances largely beyond their control, such as physical or mental disabilities, divorce, family breakdown, illness, old age, unlivable wages or discrimination in the job market. (p. 6)

In other parts of the report, Alston examined racism and other forms of discrimination, the criminalization of homelessness, the criminal justice system, voting patterns and jurisdictional gerrymandering, and other features of the US system. Finally, in his conclusions, Alston indicated that "punishing and imprisoning the poor is the distinctively American response to poverty in the twenty-first century. . . . It is difficult to imagine a more self-defeating strategy" (p. 18).

In his book, *Capitalists Arise!,* Peter Georgescu (2017) wrote, "Nearly 60 percent of the population stays afloat through deficit spending. In other words, to put food on the table and pay their bills, they have to borrow money" (p. 17). He went on to say that the bottom tenth of the population will go $15,000 deeper in debt every year. To make matters worse, structural unemployment, or a form of long-term unemployment caused by a mismatch between workers' skills and the jobs available in the market, means that there are 92 million Americans sixteen years old or older who want to work but are unable to find a job, or, in other words, a third of the employable workforce is out of work. According to a different analyst, the average US worker has less than an associate's degree, earns about $17 per hour, has a net worth of about $36,000, about $6,000 excluding home and vehicle equity, and lives "paycheck to paycheck" (Yang, 2018).

How can we employ 92 million people? Will this number grow as technology replaces a variety of current jobs? As a start, let's consider our nation's infrastructure. As Georgescu put it, there is "the well-discussed critical need for rebuilding our crumbling infrastructure in cities and throughout the rest of the country: roads, railroads, airports, bridges, the electrical grid, subways, water pipes, and more" (2017, p. 84). Here is a natural place to employ hundreds of thousands of workers to make our physical space more livable.

In light of the escalating cost of housing and the stagnation in wages, clearly one significant improvement must be made in the minimum wage. At present, $7.25 per hour is grossly inadequate for paying for housing and meeting other household expenses. Several communities are now experimenting with more than a 100 percent increase, up to $15 per hour. These pilot projects should be carefully scrutinized. If the worst fears of the opponents are not realized, there is every reason to increase the national minimum wage substantially, thus moving hundreds of thousands of households out of poverty and into greater financial security.

A recent report from the Economic Policy Institute highlighted further the economic inequalities in the United States. "Income inequality has risen in every state since the 1970s. . . . In 2015, a family in the top 1 percent nationally received, on average, 26.3 times as much income as a family in the bottom 99 percent" (Sommeiller &

Price, 2018, p. 1). As the report went on to say, this was an increase from 2013. Furthermore, "Overall in the U.S., the top 1 percent took home 22.03 percent of all income in 2015" (p. 4). This share was just slightly below the highest share ever recorded, in 1928, just before the Great Depression. (The report defines income as wages and salaries, interest from savings accounts, and capital gains.)

All in all, the UN report and the other analyses constitute a telling commentary on life in the United States. It is, indeed, a striking indictment of our economy, our society, and our culture, all of which are directly relevant to extreme poverty and homelessness today. Although our book does not address each and every issue that Alston and others examine, many are germane to our examination of homelessness, as our contributors' stories attest.

Prevention

Prevention is an area that needs major rethinking. Those experiencing homelessness today, in numbers roughly equivalent to those of forty years ago, are by and large different people from those who experienced homelessness in the late 1970s and 1980s. However, the cohort of persons experiencing homelessness is being continually replenished by those who are newly without homes. For example, in the 2017 PIT report from the Metro Denver Homeless Initiative, 80 percent of the respondents had been homeless for less than three years, and 40 percent had had their first experience of homelessness within the past three years. Almost one in five persons experiencing homelessness was "newly homeless" (Metro Denver Homeless Initiative, 2017).

In short, we have not learned how to "turn off the spigot"—to prevent people from becoming homeless in the first place. Although the federal government did allocate some funding for prevention because of the Obama stimulus package of 2009, by 2012 those extra funds had disappeared, and the federal emphasis on prevention also withered. Efforts to predict future homelessness have proved futile, and uncertainty exists as to how long we should assist an individual or family from becoming homeless. However, if we are to ever end homelessness, we must do a much better job of preventing people from becoming homeless in the first place (Evans, Sullivan, & Wallskog, 2016).

Affordable Housing

The Affordable Housing Deficit. According to the research conducted by the National Low Income Housing Coalition (2018c), there is not one state in our nation where the minimum wage pays enough to secure a modest two-bedroom apartment. Not one. The average American needs to earn an hourly wage of $21.21 an hour, or $13.96 more than the federal minimum wage of $7.25. Or they would need to work approximately 117 hours per week, the equivalent of nearly three full-time jobs, in order to rent a home at fair market value. And although the majority of hourly employees do not actually earn minimum wage—the average hourly wage is $16.38—this still puts them $4.83 an hour short of affordable rent (National Low Income Housing Coalition, 2018b). In fact, there are only twenty-two counties in the entire nation in which a worker can afford a one-bedroom unit with minimum wage (National Low Income Housing Coalition, 2018c).

As a rule, according to HUD, a household should not be spending more than 30 percent of its income on housing. For a variety of reasons, including inadequate financial resources, escalating housing costs, un- or underemployment, insufficient health care, and so on, we have large numbers of households spending well over 30 percent of their income on housing, thus putting them at significant risk of becoming homeless. Adding up all those experiencing homelessness with all those spending more than 30 percent of their income on housing, we have a deficit of about eight million affordable housing units across the country. Each state, on average, would have to create 160,000 units overnight to eliminate that deficit. Because of this, the National Low Income Housing Coalition (2018a) estimated that there are only about "35 affordable and available units for every 100 Extremely Low Income renter households" (p. 2).

Even when families are armed with tenant-based rental assistance, like vouchers, that does not mean there are landlords willing to accept vouchers or that vacant units exist in the surrounding community. Additionally, the amount approved for a voucher in a given area is based on lagging data regarding housing costs, creating a gap between the amount of the voucher and the actual market rate. This quest for affordable housing units continually forces individuals and families farther and farther away from their established network, schools, and jobs, inadvertently creating a whole new set of barriers as their natural support systems fade with each subsequent move.

An analysis conducted by the National Alliance to End Homelessness (2013) found that an average household paying for housing, called a "housing consumer," spent 27 percent of its income on housing. Among the highest 20 percent of income earners, their average annual salary was $153,300, and they spent 19 percent on housing, leaving them about $126,000 a year for everything else, or about $10,000 per month. However, the lowest 20 percent of income earners spent 87 percent of their income on housing, leaving approximately $1,310 annually for all other expenses, or a mere $109 a month for *everything else*—food, clothing, health care, childcare, transportation, and other basic essentials. In addition, the next lowest 20 percent of income earners spent 45 percent of their monthly income on housing, also leaving them at risk of homelessness. Furthermore, these statistics do not include individuals who do not have a home, since they are not considered housing consumers and, therefore, were excluded from this analysis.

Addressing the Affordable Housing Unit Gap. The government alone cannot address the problems related to inadequate affordable housing. It will require partnership with the private sector to bridge this gap. In 1986, the Low Income Housing Tax Credit (LIHTC) was created to provide tax incentives for developers to build affordable units. To date, there are approximately 2 million units nationally as a result of this program with an annual growth of around 100,000 units (National Housing Law Project, 2017). And while this type of program has been successful, this rate of growth cannot possibly keep up with demand, particularly for extremely low-income households.

Block grants are another source of public funding for affordable housing. The HOME Investment Partnerships program is a block grant to states and local jurisdictions for the creation of affordable housing, specifically to low-income households, in the form of both owner-occupied and rental units. The Community Development Block Grant is another federal grant aimed at supporting rehabilitation, revitalization, homeownership, and construction (US Department of Housing and Urban Development, 2012). While these programs do contribute to the creation of affordable units, they are subject to funding cuts and political whims at the federal level, and they are insufficient to keep pace with demand.

Housing trust funds to develop units have become another popular approach in addressing the need for more affordable housing at the city, county, and state levels. Nearly all states and over 700 cities and counties have created these funds (National Low Income Housing Coalition, n.d.). They dedicate an ongoing source of revenue for "the production or preservation of affordable housing through the acquisition, new construction, reconstruction, and/or rehabilitation of non-luxury housing" (US Department of Housing and Urban Development, 2018, para. 1).

Additionally, some areas of the country have begun developing community land trusts, which are generally nonprofits working with both public and private funding to acquire and maintain ownership of the land with the goal of assuring access to permanently affordable housing, specifically for low- or moderate-income families, like many of those able to pay for motels but unable to secure permanent housing. They are commonly referred to as shared equity programs and can vary substantially. However, they place a common focus on long-term affordability by separating the land from the structure, allowing them to lease the land to the owner of the property at no or very low cost. This keeps housing costs low indefinitely and creates community voice in the decisions regarding the property. This model is gaining traction nationally, with the largest land trust located in Vermont and overseeing thousands of owner-occupied and affordable rental units. Other regions of the country with infamous housing prices, such as New York City, Denver, and Central Oregon, are beginning to implement community land trusts as a way to stabilize the market and combat gentrification.

Although there are increasing numbers of interesting new ways to address this need, it is clear that, as a nation, we still suffer from a deplorable lack of adequate low-income housing. The 8-million-unit deficit is but one piece of evidence of that lack. In short, regardless of the method, there must be a large-scale effort comprising adequate funds and the right partners working together to address the gap.

Access to Quality Data

Quality data are essential to assure the right people are getting the right interventions at the right time. Accurate data can help identify evidence-based strategies that work and determine the effectiveness of programs created to end homelessness. Additionally, data allow the industry to make informed decisions surrounding policy and funding.

Effective use of a Homeless Management Information System (HMIS) is required for HUD funding; each Continuum of Care (CoC) program provider may select its own system to meet HUD requirements. When implemented and used appropriately, HMIS is a powerful tool for understanding the population of individuals experiencing homelessness and strategies that are working in the region, and it allows informed, data-driven decisionmaking.

Currently, data on the number of individuals experiencing homelessness are collected through the PIT count conducted in local communities at the end of January each year. While this count does provide valuable data, it is simply a snapshot of the issue and has several data quality issues. The one consistent finding from these counts is that this snapshot tends to underestimate the number of individuals experiencing homelessness, as it is often difficult to locate everyone experiencing homelessness in local communities. Conversely, a robust HMIS system with well-trained staff at local agencies inputting data can provide communities with a much more accurate picture of the overall status of homelessness, allowing the communities to track changes in the count and utilization rates of programs, and enabling them to determine the most effective methods for ending homelessness.

In order for HMIS to be maximally useful, agencies that are not receiving federal funding need to be convinced of the considerable value in using HMIS. Once all the agencies in a CoC start using HMIS, the resulting demographic data will be much more complete regarding the population experiencing homelessness, the services that are being offered, the gaps in services, and the impact of those services. Currently, there is a movement for states to adopt a uniform HMIS across all its CoCs, as opposed to each CoC's maintaining its own discrete system; this allows for a larger, uniform, statewide approach to ending homelessness.

Coordinated entry also provides another key strategy in providing access to appropriate resources, specifically housing. HUD's goal for coordinated entry is that "assistance be allocated as effectively as possible and that it be easily accessible no matter where or how people present" (US Department of Housing and Urban Development, 2017b, p. 1). Coordinated entry allows communities to assess individuals, determine their level of vulnerability, and connect them with the appropriate services to meet their needs. Additionally, by having these assessments flow through one or more coordinated entry points, the community can identify gaps in programs or resources. Effective coordinated entry systems are person-centered (i.e., the participants have choices in the types of services they access, their location, and other decisions regarding the intervention). These systems should also focus on getting individuals into housing as quickly as possible with few or no barriers or programmatic requirements, commonly referred to as housing first, discussed in the next section.

Housing First and Other Models

There are several promising federal approaches to housing those experiencing homelessness. Service delivery models such as housing first have begun to do away with requirements that could be barriers to immediate housing. As Marie said in a written statement with her implications,

> Housing first is the idea that in order for any individuals or families to move out of crisis, the housing crisis must be immediately resolved first. A housing first approach is one where families or individuals do not have to meet certain requirements to get back into permanent housing. Housing first is a model that attempts to remove as many barriers to housing as possible and meets people where they are. Several research studies have proven that housing first produces positive outcomes for individuals and families experiencing homelessness. In a community-based participatory research study on the island of Oahu, Hawaii, researchers engaged with participants who were part of a program that utilized housing first and asked participants for the ways in which housing first has changed their lives. Participants said that the housing first model was critical in helping them see the opportunity to reach their full potential and the opportunity to take care of one's self. Participants also reported improved mental health while being part of a program that had housing first as a center of their programming (Pruitt et al., 2018). Housing first projects also housed individuals and families quicker, and in some studies, contributed to families maintaining stable housing (National Alliance to End Homelessness, 2016). Traditionally, the philosophy of housing first was only thought to work in conjunction with the permanent supportive housing model, what is commonly referred to as a traditional Housing First model. In the last five years, many rapid rehousing models have also utilized housing first practices, adopting the original Housing First thinking, when structuring their programs.

> Another service delivery model that has been proven to work, and connects directly with the Housing First model, is permanent supportive housing. This is the idea that an individual or family that has high needs, high barriers to housing, and is highly vulnerable is placed into housing where they will be taken care of for as long as they need to be. Many permanent supportive housing units are designed for individuals with disabilities, who would not be able to secure or maintain stable housing on their own. Thus, when permanent supportive housing started to become funded by the Department of Housing and Urban Development in the 2000s, certain funds were given to

Continuums of Care to provide permanent supportive housing to individuals experiencing chronic homelessness (Khadduri, 2016). Since its inception, permanent supportive housing, usually coupled with intensive case management, has shown increases in the amount of time people stay housed and increased mental health wellness for individuals and families formerly without a home. In a randomized control trial of 1,198 individuals, individuals receiving permanent supportive housing services and intensive case management showed significantly greater housing stability than individuals receiving care as usual (Stergiopoulos et al., 2015).

Finally, rapid rehousing can help move individuals and families who are without a home back into a home in a very short time. Rapid rehousing is based on the premise that it is cheaper and often less traumatic to rapidly get individuals and families back into a home where they have a lease agreement than to keep them in emergency shelters or transitional housing programs (Khadduri, 2016). Many rapid rehousing programs aim to quickly stabilize individuals and families into a new home, and then provide supportive services for families moving forward to ensure they keep the place they are living. Supportive services can include anything from rental assistance to transportation assistance to connecting clients with resources and community agencies. It is important to note that unlike permanent supportive housing, which aims to connect clients to providers for as long as they need it, rapid rehousing is a short-term intervention.

Many of our resources are often dedicated to assisting once individuals and families have already lost their housing and are part of the homelessness system. In addition to providing resources to individuals and families who have already lost their housing, we should be preventing individuals and families from falling into homelessness in the first place. In addition to only serving families and individuals in leases that are at risk of losing housing with homeless prevention funds, we need to also make a decision on how to respond to the high numbers of families that are doubled up and living with friends or family or living in motels and on the brink of becoming unsheltered. Right now, what is defined as homeless changes between nonprofit agencies, service providers, and even government agencies. Programs that will consider families living in hotels/motels or families living doubled up as eligible for homeless prevention assistance are programs that meet the needs of countless families that we do not even have data on, because they are not recognized by our homeless data collection systems. Living in a hotel/motel or living with friends or family is often one of the last resorts before a family loses that support and does become labeled "literally homeless," where they face the choices of being in a shelter, in a car, or on the streets. We should have programs for families who are in this last chance/last resort scenario. Most of the time, my family lived in motels that they were paying for with their own money because my father worked as an electrician and completed side jobs to pay for them. There were no known homeless prevention or assistance programs that would provide assistance for my family to become fully housed again, as we were lost in the middle and labeled neither "literally homeless" nor "stably housed."

Housing Subsidies

When broaching the topic of housing subsidies, the discussion typically focuses on the approximately $50 billion allocated each year by HUD to support vulnerable populations with housing. However, little attention is paid to the nearly $75 billion in lost tax revenue annually as a result of the mortgage interest deduction (MID) on owner-occupied homes. This deduction only benefits individuals earning enough to itemize taxes, or generally only the top income earners. This particular economic benefit of home ownership continues to inflate housing prices in some markets, is one of the most regressive tax instruments currently in our tax code, and is fundamentally unnecessary as it is a subsidy benefiting those who need it least. If one adds in tax deductions for other kinds of taxes, top income earners receive 80 percent of federal subsidies, leaving only 20 percent for vulnerable populations. In other words, those who need the most get the least (Collinson, Ellen, & Ludwig, 2015).

During the most recent federal tax reform in 2018, there were minor changes to the MID. First, the reform package lowered the cap on the mortgage interest deduction and increased the standard deduction, meaning the estimated number of individuals itemizing and utilizing the mortgage interest deductions would decline even further, leaving only the highest income earners the ability to itemize and benefit from the deduction. However, there are still billions in lost revenue projected each year, meaning a significant net loss of tax revenue for the federal government, money being placed back into the households that need it least.

Criminal Justice Reform

Homelessness is the outcome of the failure of several systems, including the criminal justice system. In the case of Marie, warrants for failure to appear and other smaller infractions made finding secure housing significantly more difficult for their young family. For Marie's mother, an anxiety attack led to her missing a court date for a car accident and a subsequent warrant. Embarrassment over her mental health condition meant she never actually addressed the warrant. Marie's father was accused of stealing materials from a job site by a former boss, who only accused him after her father had announced he would be leaving the position. Unable to afford a lawyer, and not understanding the resources available to obtain one, Marie's father also had a warrant issued. This inhibited his ability to find work on the books, meaning he often had difficulty meeting some of the work requirements to maintain certain assistance, such as TANF. He was too scared to admit to the caseworker that he had a warrant, for fear he would immediately be arrested. Here again, unfamiliarity with this system led to consequences that followed Marie's father for years, affecting their entire family unit.

It is unfair and continually punitive to discriminate in employment and housing against those who have evictions, arrest warrants on their record, or those who have served their time in jail. Considering that the US system of criminal justice is supposed to be reformative, why do we as a society feel it necessary to continually punish ex-offenders upon their release? We strip felons of their voting rights, make it more difficult to obtain employment, and create perpetual barriers to housing by maintaining this philosophy. Additionally, by putting these barriers to employment *and* housing in place, we are inadvertently making it more likely that individuals will reoffend.

Several states and municipalities have enacted "ban the box" practices, removing the question of an applicant's arrest history from employment applications, allowing an employer to consider an applicant's qualifications independent of any criminal background information. Commonly referred to as fair-chance legislation, as of the date of this book, eleven states have passed ban the box laws for private employers. Many more states have fair-chance legislation for public sector work (Avery & Hernandez, 2018). Some cities have expanded this legislation to include housing applications as well. This is a step in the right direction, and more discussion is needed at both the state and national levels to enact these types of laws and protections for individuals reentering society.

The Role of Schools

In Marie's case, the educational system, and specifically the resources to remain in her original school while she experienced homelessness, played a critical role in her success today. Her JROTC program provided her the consistency and network she craved, and her status as homeless allowed her access to educational resources to receive transportation to her original school, suggesting public education provides a unique opportunity to break cycles and combat homelessness.

For many students experiencing homelessness, school provides the safe, stable, structured environment needed, and it is often where they feel the most supported and part of a community. It may also be the only place these students receive regular meals, as students identified as experiencing homelessness are automatically enrolled in the National Student Lunch Program, giving them access to free lunch.

Though increasing numbers of our nation's students are identified as experiencing homelessness, there is grossly inadequate funding to support their educational, social, and emotional needs. For example, under the protections provided by the Every Student Succeeds Act (2015), students experiencing homelessness have the right to receive transportation back to their school of origin, when it is in their best interest, to assure they remain stable in their educational setting during times of housing instability. However, very few school districts receive adequate funds to actually provide this service. Resources for students experiencing homelessness in public schools are mostly tied to a competitive grant process with funds flowing from the federal government, to the State Education Agency, to the districts. However, the amount of this funding is based on a state's poverty level, not the number of students identified as experiencing homelessness, and only allows for a small percentage of districts within each state to receive funding. For example, there were 17,678 school districts in the United States in school year 2016–2017. Of them, only 4,303 received grant funds dedicated for the needs of children and youth experiencing homelessness, or a mere 24 percent, creating an environment in which the rest of the districts must dip into other funding streams to provide even a basic level of support as mandated by this federal legislation (National Center for Homeless Education, 2018).

This lack of funding means school districts often perceive these statutory requirements, and what is truly in the best interest of children, as an unfunded mandate. Finding the resources to support these students in an already strapped public education budget is nearly impossible.

As stated earlier, the portion of our nation's children who experience homelessness is about 2.5 percent. In New York City, approximately one in ten students in 2014–2015 was identified as meeting the USED definition of homelessness (National Center for Education Statistics, 2017). If we were talking about anything else that affects our nation's students at this rate, something more would have already been done. But, since this is an issue of poverty, there are few rallying behind it or advocating for the resources necessary to maintain educational stability for these students.

This instability is impacting our nation's children long term. In school year 2015–2016, a mere 30.6 percent of McKinney-Vento students tested in state assessments were proficient in reading, and this percent plummeted to 25.4 percent in mathematics (National Center for Homeless Education, 2017b). For the first time, data are now being collected on graduation rates of students experiencing homelessness, which will further uncover the true challenges faced by these children and youth.

It is imperative that we understand and acknowledge the educational challenges facing students who are experiencing homelessness, using the broader USED definition. We have identified some of the specific challenges that students face, and we have described some of the approaches that are being taken to address them. This is a start, but much more needs to be done to ensure that students like Marie, and families like hers, can be truly successful.

5

A Safe Place for Youth: Tiffany's Journey

Once again, we meet a young person from a dysfunctional family. As she indicates in her story, by the age of fifteen, Tiffany had been in so many placements outside the home that she couldn't count them all, thus highlighting the importance of proper and appropriate foster care placements when a child has social or emotional needs that cannot be addressed in such facilities as juvenile detention centers or addiction treatment centers. We also see the importance of supportive, helpful school programs that can make the difference in assisting individuals to move toward self-sufficiency and away from homelessness.

Tiffany's Story

When I was four or five, I remember living at my grandmother's. It was my favorite place to live. I think my sister and I lived with Grandma for a few years, and then we went back to my mom, bouncing between different households between the ages of four and eight, from what I remember. When I moved back with my mom full-time, that's where I feel like things started to go downhill. I was eight when I went back to live with her permanently.

By this time, my mother had married a man that my sister and I didn't really have a chance to build a relationship with.

After I moved there, I started to hate school. I just felt different from the other kids around me in my new school. By fifth grade, I was already not motivated to go to class and got my first nearly failing grade. From that point on, I was on a path and just stopped caring about school. I constantly felt like I didn't belong, both at home and at school. I didn't feel like I had a relationship with my mom; although I loved her, there really wasn't a bond or a connection between us. Then, I wasn't involved much in the activities in school because even though I'd now spent three years in the neighborhood, I still didn't feel connected.

By middle school, I began to run away, and when ninth grade came, I'd been almost fully acclimated to the streets, learned how to navigate the bus system, and began to learn of places I could stay while I was gone from home. By the time I was fifteen, I had been in so many different places I'd lost count. One of the mysteries in my life is still *why*. I'm still not sure if I was removed from my home or if I didn't have an adult willing for me to live with them. One of the group homes for girls I went to thirteen different times. They were short-term. I'd go to different shelters or facilities for a few days, get a shower and food, steal some clothes, and then I would leave.

The summer I was fifteen, I tried to live with my dad while school was out. This was probably the first place I actually wanted to be in a long time. It was this summer that I realized running was how I dealt with my life. One morning, after having been there a few weeks, I came out of my room and began to walk toward the kitchen to make food, and there's my dad lying with two people on the couches. Naked. There was a guy and girl. I saw that, turned around, got some clothes on, went to his room, took all the money in his wallet, and ran. Right as I got to the door, he was there behind me. He said, "Where are you going?" I felt embarrassed, and in that moment, I knew I wasn't going to see him again. I said, "I'm leaving." It was the saddest moment for me. It was like slow motion. I tried to say it slowly, because I didn't want him to think I was mad at him. But, deep down, I think he knew I meant I was leaving for good. After that, it was as if he completely disowned me.

A year later, when I was sixteen, I went into a treatment center. I seriously had to be one of the most pitiful people in the treatment center. I was there because I would not stay still. Because I was running away so much, they needed me in a locked facility so I would stay put. They knew they needed a locked facility, but they couldn't put me in jail because I hadn't technically committed any crimes that called for jail. The plan was to be there six months, get my thyroid back on track (I have medical conditions), and work on some of my anger. It became time for me to exit the facility, and one of my treatment goals was to have family meetings, aka family group therapy. That's when I saw that my mom wasn't showing up, and in order for me to come home, she had to show up for the family group therapy sessions. The facility staff set up another family meeting, and thankfully my grandmother came! Willing to take me in, she ended up becoming a foster parent and fostering me. That was pretty awesome. It was probably the best year of my life. I got back into school, was doing ridiculously amazing, and even had a 4.0 GPA. I got into choreography, which I loved. I had friends. I got involved in church. I was in the plays, even playing the lead in one. I got a temporary job at a major performing arts center in the city. I was doing great! It was awesome, and I just flourished! I was happy.

And then, like the story of many girls, they meet a boy and lose sight of everything in front of them. At seventeen I met a guy that had been in a group home himself. He was so charming, so funny, and he swept me off my feet. We met at the drive-through where I worked. He made me feel special, not knowing that four years later I'd be victimized by his violence. He would later beat the shit out of me.

He and I lost contact shortly after we met, and I started dating someone else. He was caring, had a stable, close-knit family that I loved to be around, and at age nineteen I became pregnant. The day I told him I was pregnant on the phone, he said he'd "call me back." He never did, leaving me to face the pregnancy and parenting a child solo.

About a year later, "drive-through boy" came back into my life, and we got back together. He moved in with me. I noticed he'd changed. The charm had disappeared. It was like I didn't know this guy. He had turned aggressive. One day, after a particularly disturbing interaction with him, I called my older sister and told her a little bit of what was going on. Then I asked her if she could keep my baby because I couldn't guarantee we'd be safe at home. After dropping my daughter off, I parked practically three complexes down from my apartment so that he wouldn't see my car and know I was home. I was scared and even kept the lights off, until the morning when I had to go to work and needed to get ready.

That morning I heard him in the back yelling at me to let him in. The front door was clear, so I rushed to get my purse from the living room, and right as I went for the front door, no joke, in the matter of a minute, that man climbed up someone else's balcony, used the lid from the BBQ pit to break the bedroom window open, climbed in the bedroom from my balcony, and right as I reached to open the door, he was behind me and slammed it shut. It was over after that. He started to beat the crap out of me. I tried fighting back, but he was full of rage, making him much stronger than I was.

I remember crawling through the hallway bent over and he kicked me in my ribs. Somehow, I got to the bedroom and sat on the bed. Broken glass was on the floor from him breaking the window, and he grabbed my ankle, pulled me onto the floor, and slid my back through all that broken glass. He just kept yelling, demanding I give him my car keys. I felt trapped because no matter what I did or where I went in the house, he wouldn't leave me alone. As I sat on the couch, he began to come near me again. I screamed out the window, "Someone help me! He's beating me! Call 911!" I yelled my name out the window so they knew who I was. I think I'd seen that on *Law & Order* or something. He'd stopped hitting me by this point and was yelling at me to leave.

But, right as I got close to the front door, he did something that showed me he really wasn't going to let me go and was probably going to keep hitting me. During that moment, I felt like I had no other choice. I took one step to the kitchen and picked up a knife. I had no emotion. It was like I was okay with whatever was about to happen. And, he didn't come near me. That was pretty much my stance. If you come near me, you're gonna die. I might die, but I'm not dying without you going first. The police ended up arriving shortly thereafter, putting an end to this horrible experience.

What's unfortunate is that I didn't know how to handle the communication with the apartment manager about the situation. I was ashamed and felt it was all my fault, so I ended up leaving that apartment in a very immature way. I took some of my things and left the place in a mess. Because of the lack of communication, it turned into an eviction and high damage costs reported to the credit bureau. After I left that place, my brother let my baby and me stay at his apartment. I was still waitressing at that time, but I was working on getting into college.

For a really long time I struggled in this similar, rotating dysfunction. I found myself spiraling further and further in poverty, enduring bad relationships, mediocre jobs, low stability, more homeless shelters, and couch surfing. I used tax money to purchase cars from buy-here places, from people who knew how to rip me off, and those cars were never dependable. This cycle felt like a long, never-ending revolving door of instability coming from all different types of directions. But, in between these experiences, I was trying to teach myself how to be responsible. I had a few apartments where I learned to put a little money aside here and there to plan for next month's rent. One day, in 2011, I decided I couldn't keep going the way I was. I was living with a relative at that time and noticed how codependent I had become, and decided it was time to commit to teaching myself how to fully be an adult.

I found a cheap place to live and was upfront about my financial situation with the staff. I asked the condo manager if he would work with me on the deposit. He agreed, and we moved in. Just like that. I remember that first night. I had no furniture, food, or dishes. I took my daughter to Chipotle for dinner, and we were getting there right as it was closing. I noticed they just made a new batch of rice and I was curious, because they were getting ready to close, what were they going to do with the fresh food? The manager stated because of the laws, they have to throw it out. I don't remember what else was part of the conversation, but I remember he gave us a couple of bowls of rice. We went home full and with extra food to put in the fridge.

At the time, my daughter had a small pink tree that was a night-light. I plugged it in that night, and we lay down on the carpet, talked about the awesome experience at Chipotle, and I held her in my arms. There was so much peace in that moment because it was our home, and I knew I was going to give up all of my old habits to make a stable place for her. A place where the moment we walked in, the worries of the world stayed outside as we closed and locked our front door. It wasn't anything special, but it was a place where I knew the second chapter of my life was going to start.

In my earlier years, I had no value in higher education, no vision in life, and zero discipline. I'd gone to community college, used almost all of my lifetime financial aid award, racked up student loan debt, withdrew and failed classes, and had nothing to show for the four years I was in school. I'd been on academic probation, was eventually placed on academic suspension, and wasn't allowed to continue school until I completed certain requirements. After I got a little stable in our new place, I was able to clear up some old debt and learn time management, responsibility, and all of the things needed to be stable. I went to the "scholarship office," which was one person at the time—an amazing woman who went the extra mile to support me by telling me the tools I needed to apply for scholarships. I went to her and was brutally honest. I told her, this is who I am, this is what I've done, and I've royally screwed up in life for the last fifteen years, and I knew I needed to go back to college. I needed to start finding a way to bring a positive balance to all of this. I asked what I needed for scholarships. I remember her asking me if I had anyone that could write me a letter of recommendation. I remember laughing at my history and thinking, "You clearly didn't hear anything I just said. Maybe my old probation officer from twelve years ago . . . ?"

But, I literally had no one, nobody, who could say a good word for me. I told her I recently became involved in my church. They had this class teaching women how to become better at being a woman and a friend. It was once a week and curriculum based. I had been going every week for a few months. She told me to talk to the individual teaching the class, to see if she would write me a letter.

So, I went to the teacher of the class, face to face, and told her the same information I'd shared with the scholarship office. This is who I am, what I've done, where I'm at, and where I want to go. I asked her for a letter of recommendation for my scholarship applications, and she was so moved she almost started crying.

She was a good person. And, that's what did it. She wrote the letter to help get me scholarships, and I earned scholarships the entire time I was at the college.

Academically, during the first year I really just navigated on my own and barely used general advising to figure out my classes. My degree audit, picking classes, putting together a schedule, registering and dropping courses were mainly done on my own. For that entire year though I kept seeing signs around campus with questions on it like, "Are you the first in your family to go to college?" "Do you need support navigating?" I kept thinking, "Yes. Yes. Yes." These signs were everywhere: in bathroom stalls, on billboards, walls, everywhere. I couldn't help but see them. So, I called the program the signs were advertising. It was called TRIO, a program designed to help economically disadvantaged students who are first-generation college-goers.

This is where I met two of the people that came into my life at the right time. I filled out the application and got an interview. It was a big deal! Fast-forward, I was accepted into the program. In TRIO, you get one adviser the whole time you're in school, and I was blessed with Nnena. You get financial literacy, budgeting, education on student loan to income ratio, transfer guidance, course selection, and resourceful advice and guidance with things like problem-solving skills and managing time. My advising sessions always went deeper though. There was a lot I faced during my time there. I ended up losing my license due to a DUI, faced jail time, was homeless for a month, all while parenting my daughter.

Besides the month that I was unhoused, I pretty much lived in this two-bedroom place I got in 2011. I lived there for five and a half years. If it wasn't for them selling it, I would still be living there. I probably would have never moved because one of my goals was to work my way up to purchasing a home. It wasn't anything fancy. But, even my daughter will tell you, this was the only place that we'd walk into and go "Ahhhhh," a sigh of relief. It was home. Nothing fancy. But, it was home.

During my time in college I had work-study. I was employed in the Student Life Department. That was another place where everything changed. While I was working there, the director of the Theater Department reached out to the Student

Life Department—there were only four of us—and she asked for help with planning the open mic night. I've always enjoyed planning events, especially anything related to arts. She told us there were normally ten to fifteen people that came to open mic, and most of them were performers. But I volunteered to plan, facilitate, and see the project through. I ran with it! We had eighty people at that open mic night and twenty performers! My whole vision came to life. It was so awesome. I learned a lot from that experience. To me, it wasn't a work-study job; it was, but it wasn't. I was an adult, wanting to know adult things, and I wanted some skills. I was looking to balance out all the negative crap I had built against me, by building skills.

During school, I was named one of the annual Student Success Award recipients. There were fourteen of us. That was where I told a piece of my story for the first time. The Marketing Department asked us to write our own bio, and he said that most people set up a time to talk with him, and then the guy in communications usually put it together as most people don't want to write. I decided to write my own. I was crying when I wrote it. I had talked a little bit about it in my scholarship essays. But, by this time, I was a year into college and being successful. I was learning all these skills, making connections. I felt like I had a different outlook. As I started to write it, the words turned into tears, which turned into therapy, and I just kept writing. And I sent it to him that day, asking him what he thought of my draft. He told me to "keep it" and not change a word. And so, it got published on the website—the main website. We each had our own picture on the front page. And that's when it became real. On the internet. It was there. I have to say, the story from years ago is different than it looks now. There was a lot of bitterness at that point in my life. I was angry still. I was still pretty pissed off at people.

I had a year left in school, and I was finding that one of my favorite things to do was check my degree audit because my percentage would go up, moving me step by step closer to graduation. I hadn't figured out what I wanted to do yet though, even with graduation approaching. It was that summer when I came running into the TRIO office to tell my adviser, "OMG I know what I want to do!" I want to study sociology. It was because of the following experience I'd had.

There was this old apartment that I had been living in for ten months. I went to the apartment manager and told her that I lost my job. She and I worked out an agreement to get out of the lease. They mailed my balance to the wrong address, and we got it worked out after about two months. But by then, the apartment complex was trying to come after me for over $1,800, when I really only owed about $400. They ended up putting me in collections for the $400, but when I'd get my bill each month, even though I'd paid a substantial amount, the balance didn't reflect it. I'd spend my lunches, breaks, spare time trying to figure it all out. But, there was money disappearing. I asked for my ledger to see where this money was going, and none of it added up. I finally told them I wasn't paying them any more. I'd owed them $400 and had already paid over $500. We should be even. None of it was adding up. I still had a $128 balance left, and I refused to pay it. Within a week or so, someone showed up at my job and served me with papers to sue me for the full $1,800.

I represented myself in court. It took me months to do research and figure out everything I needed to know. I had to gather documents so I could show my side of the story. Their lawyer thought I was a lawyer. I bought a really nice, cheap suit, but it fit me well. That's that cultural capital right there. I had a black bag for all my documents on me. I even learned how to file certain court documents. For example, when you're sued, you have to file a response, and I learned how to do that. The lady at court was very supportive. I told her I didn't know what I was doing, but I'm representing myself and she gave me pretty good guidance and deadlines that were helpful. I went into court and did my thing. I was actually a little excited, because I was going to cross-examine a witness. It felt like an episode of *Law & Order*.

I practiced how to ask questions in a courtroom. All my questions, which I'd written down as she was speaking, led up to me proving that the apartment manager was lying on the stand. And I won. As a side note, a friend of mine had the exact same experience. It was the same complex, the same lawyer, same law firm. It took her a few years to fight them back, but when she finally decided to, she came to ask me what to do. I gave her guidance on how I handled it, step by step of what I'd done, and she won! That's when I knew I wanted to study sociology.

My experience was in and of itself enough, but then I walked out of the courtroom that day and saw the other people that appeared to be in a similar vulnerable situation as I was with a lack of knowledge—some were English-as-a-second-language learners, some older people, and there were really young people who weren't dressed for the culture of court.

Later that year, I graduated with an associate's degree and immediately began pursuing my bachelor's degree in sociology.

The Future

After I graduate from school next year, I'm also not certain what I'll do. But, literally just the other day, I got scared. The real world. With a degree. And while I've accomplished a lot, this is just a different type of accomplishment. I'm nervous about all that. I haven't thought about what I'm going to do afterwards. I know I built a name for myself at my community college. I enjoy fighting and advocating, teaching and giving tools. I thought about law school, but I don't want to take out more loans. Maybe I'll go back and work for a program like TRIO. I've always wanted to do that, but at the same time, do I want to get out of this space? I envision myself doing something similar to what I did with my friend, helping her fight the apartment complex, guiding and encouraging others to the point where they believe in themselves.

Thoughts on How This Experience Has Affected Me

I am breaking the mold. I'm being rebellious, but in a good way. The experience of having to represent myself in court, that could have gone completely differently. What if I didn't try? If I didn't have the courage to fight for myself, I'm not sure how that would have affected me. From another perspective, my life experiences have drastically changed my parenting. The one thing that I have always been consistent about is sharing my mistakes with my daughter. And being so open with her and letting her know that stuff out there is real. Letting her know, you can do it on your own, but it's a lot harder. Life is more joyful when you have somebody crying with you in the hard times and when you get through it, celebrating together. Recognizing the responsibility of being the leader of the home, showing her how to be humble and apologize, how to forgive, not hold grudges, communicate, and work through conflict are huge skills and necessary tools. Those were all things that I had to teach myself, and truthfully, some of them I was learning while teaching her at the same time. I realized they all tied into homelessness. All of them.

There's more than one way to experience poverty, and poverty caused my experiences of homelessness. Not poverty in the sense of a lack in finances, but the lack in parental love, sense of belonging, tools, boundaries, discipline, and health. I believe there are many other people that have a similar story. Not just stories of how we have been victims of trauma and prey to those who pounce on the vulnerable, but also stories of warriors and overcomers. There's a narrative that's being repeated in organizations, programs, higher education . . . and in movies, music, and in the media. This narrative says that those of us who are poor and caught in the realm of poverty are not capable of coming out of it. It's not so. We are so capable. We need genuine partnerships, relationships, and tools. And I also think that sometimes in life barriers are systemic, and sometimes they're self-inflicted. Programs and institutions should use wisdom when addressing these barriers.

Implications

Alternative Placements

At the core of Tiffany's difficulty was once again family dysfunction and a child welfare system ill-equipped to place her in a setting that would address her specific needs. Since Tiffany's interaction with child welfare, there have been substantial changes and legislative updates to recognize a larger array of placement options. Title IV-E of the Social Security Act requires that preference be given to relatives over a caregiver who is not related. While the definition of the term *relative* varies from state to state, forty-eight states currently have statutory language regarding this requirement (Children's Bureau, 2018). Additionally, there is more attention being paid to what are commonly referred to as "fictive kin" or "a person who is not related to the child by blood, marriage, or adoption but who is known to the family" (Children's Bureau, 2018, p. 2). Twenty-eight states have this type of placement as a resource when a relative cannot be located or when no suitable one is available.

This shift is encouraging, particularly given the overarching negative outcomes for children placed in foster care versus some type of kinship care. A policy report issued by the Annie E. Casey Foundation (2012) found that "one in 11 children lives in kinship care at some point before the age of 18," and that "one in five black children spends time in kinship care" during childhood (p. 2), or about 4 percent of the overall number of children in this country and approximately 26 percent of the population of children in foster care.

This type of arrangement was found to decrease the amount of trauma a child experiences as a result of parental separation, allowing children to potentially maintain community and family connections, and create heightened stability and identity during a troublesome time. Kinship placements result in fewer behavioral issues and lower rates of psychiatric disorders. They also experience fewer school transitions, leading to increased achievement and higher school success (Annie E. Casey Foundation, 2012).

While these arrangements can have significant outcomes for children, it does disproportionately place a strain on some of the most at-risk populations of adults. These caregivers typically have higher rates of poverty, are older, possess less education, and have higher rates of unemployment (Annie E. Casey Foundation, 2012). They may be unprepared for the overwhelming amount of care these children may require, particularly when faced with multiple siblings at once.

In February 2018, the Family First Services Prevention Act was passed in a bipartisan effort to reform the funding streams of the child welfare system. This act allows Title IV-E and Title IV-B of the Social Security Act funding to be utilized for prevention services for a child who may be at risk of entering the child welfare system, and for services such as mental health treatment, parenting classes, and substance use treatment. Additionally, it gives states an incentive to reduce the number of children already in care who are placed in congregate care, as Tiffany was, which are placements with twenty-four-hour supervision like group homes, residential treatment facilities, and other types of highly structured placements (Torres & Mathur, 2018).

College Assistance for Students
Experiencing Homelessness

Beyond the K–12 system discussed in the last chapter, support at the college level is critical to students finishing their education and breaking cycles of poverty. Tiffany found a home at her campus's TRIO program, which is designed to support students who are first-generation college-goers, economically disadvantaged, or individuals with disabilities in completing their education.

Homelessness is a growing issue on college campuses. Goldrick-Rab, Richardson, and Hernandez (2017) found that approximately 13 percent of community college students are experiencing homelessness. This number climbs to 29 percent for youth who were formerly in foster care, like Tiffany. Without the familial support provided to many of their peers, these students face significant economic and emotional barriers while attempting to complete higher education.

College campuses are beginning to recognize the issue and fight back. For example, Kennesaw State University, located in Kennesaw, Georgia, was among the first in the nation to create its Campus Awareness, Resource, and Empowerment (CARE) Services, a dedicated spot for students experiencing homelessness, food insecurity, or foster care. It offers a food pantry, individualized support, housing, job placement, and assistance with scholarships, and it hosts several awareness events throughout the year, including a Homelessness Awareness Week. These wraparound services help ensure that students have food, toiletries, housing when dorms close, assistance in paying for school, and countless other supports to help them successfully navigate and complete their education.

At a macro level, states and institutions of higher education across the nation are implementing a single point of contact (SPOC) model to enhance collaboration and support as students experiencing homelessness transition from public school to postsecondary education. This movement materialized from a joint task force in Colorado dedicated to meeting the needs of unaccompanied homeless youth. The SPOC model designates one individual at the institution of higher education to assist unaccompanied students experiencing homelessness in accessing financial aid, navigating admissions, and connecting with supports on campus. This system serves as a warm handoff between the public schools and higher education as a way to assist student transition and success.

This is an important start. Not only should we be creating more opportunities for these secondary students to enroll in higher education or other postsecondary institutions, but we must provide more support for them when they arrive on campus. These students have experienced untold trauma throughout their lives, and it is incumbent on us to provide safe, secure, stable places for them through their postsecondary careers.

Eviction Prevention

Formal evictions have long-term effects for individuals seeking stable housing. As we saw in the previous chapter, Marie's parents lost housing as she entered high school, and with both of them having evictions on their records, stable housing became impossible. In this chapter, we see how a domestic violence situation led to shame, the inability to face a landlord, and subsequently to an eviction that stayed with Tiffany for years. Additionally, her story represents the difficulty tenants face with the legal system in general and why evictions continue to plague renters nationally. Some cities have begun ensuring the right to counsel to fight evictions, which follow tenants for years and are sometimes filed unlawfully. Without proper representation, many tenants simply fail to appear, creating an easy victory for landlords. This eviction generally remains on an individual's credit history for seven years, making it difficult to obtain everything from housing to loans, perpetuating the cycle of poverty and homelessness.

The need for adequate legal representation is an altogether familiar story in the homelessness arena. As Matthew Desmond (2016) describes in his groundbreaking book, *Evicted*, eviction from public housing and from private units made available through housing vouchers is a frequent occurrence. According to Desmond, "Legal aid to the poor has been steadily diminishing since the Reagan years and was decimated during the Great Recession. The result is that in many housing courts around the country, 90 percent of the landlords are represented by attorneys, and 90 percent of the tenants are not. . . . But when tenants have lawyers, their chances of keeping their homes increase dramatically" (2016, p. 303). Therefore, we must figure out a way for tenants to have access to adequate legal representation.

Other cities have passed local ordinances that forbid landlords from asking for information about the source of a potential tenant's income, Denver being one of the most recent. It is well-known that many potential landlords refuse to rent to persons with any type of federal or state housing assistance voucher because of possible delays in receiving rent payments and the possible nonpayment by the tenants themselves. These local ordinances are intended to equalize the playing field for people trying to escape homelessness.

Another effort to assist tenants is the utilization of formal documents known as mutual lease rescissions (MLRs). According to a senior staff member at the Colorado Coalition for the Homeless, in cases where a tenant is facing eviction from a unit, both the tenant and the landlord can sign an MLR, thus eliminating an eviction from the tenant's record. Although the tenant will have to leave that unit, at least there is no eviction on his/her record (C. Craig, personal communication, September 20, 2018).

Some cities and nonprofit organizations have initiated landlord recruitment efforts to identify landlords who will work with them to help place tenants. This approach is being utilized intentionally to overcome landlord fears of potentially "bad" tenants. In one case, the landlord recruiter not only works with landlords, but she acts as an ombudsman between the tenant and the landlord (C. Blair, personal communication, August 16, 2018). Just as the developmental disability community uses job coaches to assist employees in their employment situations, perhaps we need to be thinking about a whole new role, that of housing coaches, to assist tenants in their new housing situations.

We applaud all these efforts to level the playing field for individuals trying to escape the throes of homelessness. In short, we must do much more to assist them in accessing adequate and appropriate housing.

Caring Individuals

As Tiffany said,

> The first thing the world needs to know is that people are capable. That to instill dignity is huge. It's the voices of our society that I really believe hinder an individual until that individual can become old enough to realize that they can break out of that. But, what if a person never realizes that? Or, what if they know it and they're just scared to move forward because of fear? It's just so debilitating sometimes. And, I just believe sometimes it's one person that can provide someone the freedom to make their decision, but also provide guidance.

Tiffany identifies two caring people who were instrumental in her life: her grandmother and a staff person at school, Nnena. Her grandmother, Elaine, was particularly helpful when Tiffany was a teenager: "She provided the space for me to flourish." Nnena was there for her when she enrolled at the community college: "It was just she'd never kick you when you were already down." As Tiffany said,

> Just the other day, I was like, I just wish I had an adult I could call. It was Grandma, or while I was in school, Nnena. If it was during school hours I could drop by and get some advice. On the weekends I could call my grandma, and I knew that the one thing I would never hear back from either of them was, "Well, you got yourself into it," or anything along those lines. I've heard that my whole life. And even if nobody actually said it directly to me, the way that the system is, the way that it's set up. It's punitive.

Similar to what we saw earlier in Tim's chapter, placement with a caring individual makes a world of difference in the life of a child. In Tiffany's case, she had a stable relative willing to undergo foster care parent training to take custody of her, giving her stability and a place to flourish during a critical time in her life.

Tiffany went on to say,

> I mean, I experienced some stuff when I was in TRIO at my community college. Like I said, I caught a DUI, lost my license for a year and a half, literally ended up riding my bike between campuses and my job. And, still going to school, still working, still parenting, still making mistakes. But at the same time, I had a support system there to pull me out, just to give me perspective, or give me a safe space to come and cry and talk about how hard things are. A place where they could give you tools. "I hear you that this is hard, but have you thought about this? Or maybe this?" Or, to even challenge me when I told them where I wanted to go for my bachelor's. By that time, I wanted to try Harvard or Yale, or all these places that the world told me I couldn't go. Nnena supported that, but not in a way that was unrealistic. She was like, okay, here are these tools, here's this website, look here for this, Google this, and then let me know what you find. It's not that she "empowered" me. She didn't give me power. I already had my own power. She gave me the tools. You develop your own way of thinking when people give you tools. You learn to do it yourself, instead of fitting this poverty narrative and conforming to it.

As is true for several of our contributors, caring individuals, whether they are family members, teachers, guidance counselors, or other program staff, prove to be essential at critical junctures in the lives of those experiencing homelessness. This human contact, the help and guidance, the support, can mean the difference between success in moving out of homelessness and remaining a captive of a terrible situation. The importance of these caring individuals cannot be overstated. Therefore, we must develop more strategies to create these kinds of lifesaving anchors in the lives of all those experiencing homelessness, but especially for students.

6

The Foster Care System: Blizzard's Journey

With Blizzard, we see another story of a teenager with a very difficult home life, a stint in jail, and an unsatisfactory foster care situation. He even titles that part of his story "Fostering UnCare." Fortunately for him, he eventually made his way into life with three different families for short periods of time where he found time to heal from his ragged teenage years. His account provides us with an opportunity to examine foster care, its impact on the lives of youngsters, and its relationship to homelessness.

Blizzard's Story

Home is core to our humanistic desires; it's our version of the wild animal's den, nest, territory, burrow, cave—our ritualistic habitat is one place you can truly be you. I want to control the noise; I want to be naked to bathe. Home is where we recoup from all the stimuli of the world. It's my medicine when I'm tired, confused, sad, angry, sick—a personalized house is where I can celebrate by dancing, make love, take my time taking a dump, and know the cleanliness of the floor. Shelter protects me from the constant wind; walls and roof protect me from not feeling like I'm ready to die due to the extreme wild winter weatherization, which woefully wreaks my wanderlust. Home is more than walls, ceiling, heat, coolness, food, kitchen, bed, storage, safety, hobby place, mild hospital; home is a sanctuary, recharge, relation space, parenting place, memorabilia headquarters, freely cry quarters, rowdy spot, and quiet comforting den.

Initial Conditions Leading to No Nest

I was awoken by my older abandoned siblings. Before my first breath, the flames with family were melted, scarred. My biological father was a coward in the first round of creating and sustaining life; he abandoned his first child and fled the state never to return to live in it. It's hard to say if there were more children. I'm his third; he was around a little less than two-thirds of my life. Seven years of my childhood he was a ghost; he would transpose into his human form occasionally, such as rustically lawn mowing and leaving, a few letters to foster care, some Saturdays, and a jail visit that led me to the suicide tank. While we were away, I believed in his existence, while he remained a mysterious illusive man. His family crime was a lack of commitment toward his children. So, the reality is my father left me alone for 365 (when I was three) + 372 (foster care) + 678 (single mom), a Halloween season, et cetera . . . days when I was living mostly with my mother; the other times I was kicked out, ran away, or simply had no desire to be at this love-lacking, deprived of happiness family house: 1,420+ days absent.

He was lost in the world of lust and lack of commitment from the start with my biological mother. Whether he was toasting at my uncle's wedding and "hittin'" on women, or cheating with other ladies at his workplace, he was not parenting me or modeling a loving, devoted, and engaged spouse and father. At some point, my mother cracked. Through the years, she racked up a list of men she called boyfriends and got pregnant. This all occurred while they were married!

Precipitation

My parents did not open up about their problems with our extended kin, community, school, mental health professionals, jails, psychiatric facilities, and so many more social spheres. I eavesdropped a few times. They wished that I was like my older brother, an easy, familiar puzzle piece. They talked of staying together until the children were eighteen. Mainly, it was my fault; they told others about my school faults, temporal character limitations, and suicidal ideations. Apparently not enough about their own. One smart person near our family witnessed the neglect, treachery, and how I was less while my three-year-older brother was more. I felt it; I wept.

My parents abandoned me in the system. According to records, my parents were seeking to pause parental rights when I was fourteen. A year and a half later, I burglarized a home with another in search of a gun to die. A child needed a total of three felonious adjudications to be removed from the home. My mother and father could not care for themselves; they told Human Services they could not take care of this Wild Boy. They told others I was a criminal and out of control. Fuck you, Dad and Mom; all three of us are criminals! Fuck the World! "FTW" was self-inflicted on my knuckles at the tender age of fifteen while incarcerated in a "boy's group home." Tattoos were a culture of incarceration, passion, and an attempt to identify when all pillars were toppled.

For a month, I had to wait in jail for an extended, unnecessary period of time. Prior, I lived with my girlfriend at her friend's house for three months, in parks and other kids' houses. Damn, I just wanted to be left alone from them! Time marched ever so slowly in jail. I made some friends, feared others, smuggled in toothpaste as a dessert, used it to plug up the microphone to talk at night, witnessed and threatened with violence, lived like a zombie in solitary confinement for three days because I was throwing the caulking from the window at my roommate buddy, read books, slept on the floor due to overcrowding, and took note of the disproportionate minority confinement injustice, while feeling anesthetized.

Fostering UnCare

Then, I was free to leave to the foster care boys' group home, as long as I cut my long rat's tail in the back and foot-long bangs up front—punk rock hairdo! During my first night's sleep

I was rapidly awoken by a kid on my top bunk being maliciously beaten by another boy. He attacked him in his sleep! No one stopped it; no one got in trouble. I knew I lived in a den of mountain lions—ROAR! They forced us into the dark, dank, dirty basement of an old small farmhouse. Twelve boys total, ranging from fourteen to eighteen years old, four rooms. Two houseparents living upstairs, along with their adolescent sons, who we rarely saw. The door was locked to get to them, the kitchen, a phone. All the other doors were locked with alarms. The man of the house was okay, caring in his way. Often, we were left alone. He would always appear like a lightning bolt, hunting to discover ill behavior. We had weekly chores and restitution labor: cooking for sixteen, laundry for twelve, heavy rock removal in the "back forty" cow pasture via wheelbarrow, and body work on cars. There were two tiny, tight vertical showers, two toilets, and two sinks.

When the houseparents left early Friday and returned late Sunday, a whole gamut of adults came to our house. For many months, one man who was our parent was the most stout, cool, kind, and strong father figure. He once played for the NFL, culturally astute, knew how to connect, helped us navigate, and was thankfully black. Other adults flowed through and out. One young military bozo talked up his veteran status; I told him, "Fuck your war, killer; get out of my house!" Never saw the military murderer again. Another couple was straight up eerie and did not trust us. One night, the group home parents' large birds were found decapitated; he sat in the chair, all night, in front of our beds and tugged on his cigarette smoke, staring at us, so horrifically! I thought maybe he was a boy killer.

We figured a way to deactivate the alarms, so we could get liberty late at night. I made a good friend. We talked, comforted each other, tattooed, listened to music, laughed lots, hung out on the occasional free time at the gas station, music shop, and bowling alley. Then, he left. It was never the same. Kids were always disappearing, escaping, and getting arrested. I went into hibernation for the remaining months. Slept two-thirds of the day because my GED studies in a room left alone gave me ample time to sleep under the desk. On the outside, only one old friend stayed in contact with me; all the others just evaporated. When it was time to start preparing to end the conviction sentence,

I would be going to a new community. The counselor called my mom and said your son is ready to come home. My now divorced, unemployed, moved, depressed single mother stated, "He is? But, I'm not ready!" My dad, da hooker, was with a new family. I'm now sixteen, almost seventeen. My new options were go to school or get a job. I got a job at a restaurant for nine months. I did not use drugs. It was not okay, yet it was better. No other options were processed, no transitional support was present, no family counsel, and no vocational navigation!

We were all almost drained. My new room was a dark basement. Occasionally on weekends, my carcass dad would pick me up with his new unapologetic, flat, cold wife; it SUCKED! The grade got steeper! My mom would sometimes kick me out; my dad was not helpful. Our old dog that my dad abandoned along with us was shitting on my mom's bed; she was freaking out. I pushed my dad out. I was overwhelmed by racism, and action-oriented solutions were not enough; neo-Nazis were too present and violent. She'd power trip me; I threatened her once. She told me to leave; I packed my bags. I was so fucking ready to unplug from society; I'll go live and die outside. She calls them her turbulent times.

Public Relations and Life on the Streets

My love and smoothness with connecting with others, along with my nice and neat character, allowed me to make friends with females working at gas stations, ice cream stores, pizza shops, twenty-four-hour photocopy businesses, twenty-four-hour restaurants, music/book stores, and so on, which allowed me to draw, eat, recharge, get free food, sleep, read, plan, and place suicide to the side. I had virtue; I abstained from sex, and I helped other runaways go home or survive.

Within the long hallways of a grocery store strip mall lay malnourished night owls, hooting under the lamp of night and yearning to be free of this winter struggle. My younger runaway best friend, often, where the graveyard shift occupied the confines, would break down theory and create solutions around social justice and environmental issues with me. On one of the many blandly painted benches bolted to the colorless tile, we sat. Often, I'd eloquently declare my Fourth Amendment right to police when they rudely wanted to search me; usually, they stopped.

Sleep in the day some, awake all night. One episode of my life, I was denied a place to live, for the cool and attractive young lady I was staying with really wanted to sexually sleep in the same bed, mother approved! Illegal habitats were newspaper recycling bins, fields, golf courses, or a boiler room, on a Christmas tree, is where I'd rest my head some. Similar to most places, I had to enter late and leave early if I did not want to disturb the housed, get the pigs called, or simply lose my floor space. Here's how it went down: maybe after pretending I was using the phone in a restaurant entrance, chilling at Subway where my girlfriend worked or hangin' with someone, maybe even at their house, I'd go hunt for sleep around 11:30 p.m.

I would smoothly, like I lived there or was visiting, steadily walk right into the apartment laundry room and lock the door. I always hoped no one would do a lame-ass laundry load at 1:00 a.m. Did I ever take my Docs (boots) off? Once. Even with a cheap-ass lock, I was still concerned about runnin' in the middle of my sleep! I curled up. My one blanket was a little throw blanket to cover your legs, so I put it on the white, cold tile for cushion and warmth. I had no top blanket. It was so much better than the rooftop buildings, the cramped space hidden behind the Christmas donation box, the long sleepless nights at the ever-open diner, or in an ice box of a car, half awake—I never slept like I used to sleep at home. Prolonged poor sleep hygiene harmed my mind and body.

The sun rose. Some organized fool came in at 6:13 a.m.; he was pissed I was in there making a mess. I hauled out of there! I was paranoid this self-focused, disgusted, young dude would call the black and white. The next apartment over, to lose my homeless identity, I tossed my little blanket in a young friend's back porch. Damn, I was now back to the snow, and I was cold, mutha fuckin' cold, wintery cold, frozen, cold, COLD! Get noticed = lose your spot; get caught = get a criminal ticket. Don't show up and pay the court, you are now a criminal with a warrant for jail. The Eighth Amendment "prohibits . . . excessive fines, or cruel and unusual punishment."

On the start of my last teenage year, I again pierced my flesh. I branded myself for life by declaring "WHY" on my wrist.

Why do I feel this way, why do you treat me this way, and why does the world operate this way? While in county jail, which is where most of us get herded, due to the soulless philosophy of private property and trespassing, I bashed my head on the wall post dual-parental visit. I boggled my mind in the aquarium, aka the suicide tank in the mass jail basement. Supernatural came to me; I responded to the Great Spirit's Christ. Multiple times, I got free. In the last season, though we had a sheet of acid (100 doses of LSD), I began to lose peace and gain clarity, for I no longer wanted others to consume poison, acid rain, or the acidity of a crass society.

At summer midnight, the door to the laundromat would automatically lock. Now, I, we, were safe on the inside. I stayed there some nights, after my friends were done hanging out playing pirated video games. Eventually, I worked at the laundromat for a sleeping quarters in the stank mechanical backroom for a month. I showed up to work late once, so the boss called the pigs! My next plan was to live in the wonderful mountains and die in the blizzard of winter.

Three Families Providing Time to Heal

Because of my teenage friends, three stout, loving, radical families invited me into their homes over a course of approximately thirteen months.

Many weeks/maybe more than a month: My younger sweet teen friend had me live with her and her grandparents, Japanese/Spanish/American, and provided me my own room over a short summer. I quit work at the city art center due to my paranoia of my warrants for arrest in the same city and county. I processed, hung with my lil' sista, read books, and slept to rebuild. Understandably, they kicked me out due to me attempting to move marijuana.

Eight months: The second family was the United Nations of homes; all races and countries represented—black, Hebrew, Lakota, Peach, Mexican moto gangz, Samoan, Christian . . . my young buck brother, fellow drug user, slinger invited me to his single mom's house. My mom kicked down two months' rent at $200 for a corner in the unfinished basement. My faith in the Supreme grew as I read, worked under the table, talked with my new surrogate mom, played with the children, finished my court community service, began talking to my people who were still ill, turned myself in, and with a pocket full of cash bailed myself out to prepare liberty from the system. The judge said I'd be back if I was lying about my new life, so he dropped the eighteen months in prison and much of the restitution if I got my GED. My heart, with Spirit, agreed I needed to move farther away from the youthful drug violence in the home.

Four months: I went to live with a loving Mexican familia, single mother, whom I worked for under the table. I paid a few hundred a month for a room. It was a time to volunteer, save money at my new job of factory work, encourage/model righteousness to my old crew, and trace amounts of spent time with my mother, shards with my father. I was now really ready to live solo, financially and spiritually secure.

After I got my GED, two days a week I went to college. I'd bike, walk, skate to work and the store to honor and experience the earth. A far community away, I moved into a humble studio apartment complex, for just shy of three years; I was so grateful. My own den allowed me to be safe, creative, helpful, and prayerful. Steadily farther away from my old context, limited DNA family interface, and a steady dose of caring for my neighbors, allowed me to thrive in church community committing to Christ! I cleaned a geriatric neighbor's bathroom, paid other neighbors' rent, befriended a single mom, and got prayer from a man without a home I housed during a blizzard. It was mountainously ultra-fascinating! Not only a stable home, which seems so weak, compared to the newer human I was richly cultivating for myself. I traversed and catapulted my spiritual character past having a home and resources.

For three years, I worked at a factory with intriguing internationals from Friday to Sunday, eleven-hour shifts. I volunteered one day a week for a prisoner reentry program and cleaned for a teen/pregnant/homeless kitchen! I continued to construct blueprints for reparations toward a more balanced union. Return their sacred national parks, national forests, and/or BLM land back to Native Americans. Apologetic solution-oriented actions could be to provide African Americans forty acres of land as white landowners die or backpay the $1.7–$6.4 trillion never paid during the 250 years of unpaid slave labor.

Years went by, as I ate fresh vegetables, fruits, and rice. I denied vanity, materialism, greed, sex, ego, and alcohol—FTW. The Messiah said, "You must live in the world, yet you must not be of the world!" FTW (Flee the World). I then left the state and donated a year of my life to full-time volunteerism with AmeriCorps NCCC (National Civilian Community Corps) to serve homeless youth and environmental outdoor efforts; it was such a rad year with loads of young, altruistic people. I fell in love with a selfless, neat, fun, smart, foxy woman; we got married! Her past context was overall pretty healthy; we complement each other very wonderfully. Our kids are kind, creative, giving, neat, smart, and aware. I've been helping kids without nests and dismantling the system of oppression ever since. With poverty-level incomes, we've donated over $75,000.

For decades, I've volunteered for Earth and earthlings and worked as a holistic master practitioner of social work and a leader for youth/families in conflict, acting on solutions locally, state-wide, and nationally through me, others, organizations, and civil rights laws. I once got a state award for one who was homeless and now making it less. I declared in the microphone, "It's not simply choices. CONTEXT CREATES CHOICES!"

I have scars and open wounds from the past and now. Eight years ago, I scouted for my oldest brother; we were united. He is DNA, rad with me, and his mohawk! My sister recently sought my mother through Human Services. My persistent voice declaring how we must find and live life with my older sister came true. We were recently so happily united. Through awkwardness, joy, and pain, my siblings and I lovingly connecting from afar, as half of life has already passed. Each of them is not personally known by their biological fathers. My sister shared how I have it worse. She was left behind once, and she moved on. I was and am consistently part of my parents' lifelong struggle.

From the evolving age of twelve, I was thankfully in systems and other family homes with care from Native, African, Asian, and Latina/o Americans. United, my cellmates, foster care roommates, homeless homies, psych ward and solitary confinement neighbors were Laotians, skinheads, rural mountain Apache Mexicans, inner-city black best friends, hippy kids, CMG Blood, Wigga Crip, and sexually abused teen cowboys.

During my time without a bathroom, I lost four teeth and got a bridge (replaces a lost tooth) and a root canal, got eighteen cavities, and developed periodontal disease, which cost me more hours and dollars than most each year. Twenty-plus years later, impeding my volunteerism and vocation, I have a criminal background due to sleeping (trespassing), medicating/recreating/marketing (marijuana twice), advocating (resisting arrest, trespassing, and disorderly conduct. PIG BEAT ME UP! Later, in the holding cell, an undercover detective PSYCHOLOGICALLY TRAUMATIZED me by SCREAMING HE WILL KICK MY ASS, TEAR THE SHIT OUT OF ME IF I DON'T CONFESS TO CRIMES NOT MINE!), playing/misjudging (felony/misdemeanor plastic squirt gun. Cops lied on the report and stated it was real! Judge corrected to misdemeanor).

Verbal deficits, low self-esteem, resistant, angry, oppositional, unmotivated, and depressed were my initial diagnoses from one psychiatrist. As a youth, my parents' diagnoses would have been spiritual deficits, sexual addictions, ego over humility, conduct disorder, lack of impulse control, attention deficit disorder, selfishness, and imbalanced preference to one child syndrome. Mask off! I often was still kind, still interested and interesting, and I continuously dreamed, blissfully. My success is unity, art, flowering ultra-adventure, so your success of a mathematical equation, gaining riches, producing ego is a steady mining of the soul sold, where nothing is sacred. Mentally, I still deal with my family pushing much on me. "Get over it! They tried with you! You were difficult! Take responsibility!" my brother barks at me, decades later, knowing little my perspective, which engineers deep family dearth to generations. They seem cursed by a wicked, encapsulating spell. It is super annoying. Cage, burn, run, and pray out the darkness. Thankfully, Creator knows and heals. I am an avatar. I forgave; I have not forgotten.

Implications

Foster Care Reform

Blizzard's experience in foster care raises serious questions about our current foster care system. One of the best predictors of future homelessness is living in foster care (Baum & Burnes, 1993, p. 50), or as

Tobin and Murphy (2016) state, "Systems youth . . . are unemployed, often lack a permanent residence, and spend significant amounts of time without shelter" (p. 39).

Recent empirical studies have reinforced these statements. Dworsky, Napolitano, and Courtney (2013) found in their large study of midwestern young adults who had been in foster care that, by the time these young adults had reached the age of twenty-six, 36 percent had experienced at least one episode of homelessness since leaving their foster care placement (cited in Shah et al., 2017). A 2009 study by Fowler, Toro, and Miles found that 43 percent of their sample experienced homelessness within two years of leaving foster care. In their own empirical study of Washington State young adults, Shah and her colleagues (2017) found that 28 percent of the sample of over 1,200 young people had experienced homelessness in the first year after leaving foster care. They also identified factors that were highly correlated with post-exit homelessness. These included housing instability prior to exit, frequent school moves, numerous congregate care placements, being a teen parent, and being a person of color.

One expert on foster care provided additional insights into issues with the system. "In the past, there has been little effort to help young people in foster care develop connections outside the system itself" (K. Myers, personal communication, October 25, 2018). Young people in foster care often experience high school mobility due to frequent changes in placement. In Colorado, students in foster care move schools more often than placements (Clemens, Klopfenstein, Tis, & Lalonde, 2017). Recent federal and state school stability laws aim to bring the child welfare system and educators together to work on behalf of the young person in foster care and reduce the number of school changes. The Every Student Succeeds Act, passed in 2015, includes specific provisions aimed at keeping students in their school of origin regardless of foster placement changes. The child welfare system and education system are now equally responsible for ensuring students stay in their school of origin (when at all possible) regardless of what is happening in their home lives.

School instability has academic and social consequences, particularly for young people in foster care. Academically, students in foster care enter the child welfare system behind their nonfoster peers in reading and math (Clemens, Klopfenstein, Lalonde, & Tis, 2018). Additionally, the odds of graduating with their peers drop dramatically with every school move; on average, students in foster care move schools three times (Clemens, Helm, Myers, Thomas, & Tis, 2017). The current graduation rate for students in foster care is 23 percent, which is far below the Colorado state average of 79 percent, a trend found not just in this state, but nationally.

Social implications are also a factor for young people in care. Each placement change and school move results in a young person's being in the position to form new relationships with caregivers, peers, and school personnel. Oftentimes, students disengage in school or simply give up as a result (Clemens, Helm et al., 2017). Without a high school diploma and social connections, youth have limited options when leaving care. Not having a high school diploma or GED means a student is not eligible to go on to postsecondary education programs that include housing such as two-year or four-year colleges. Employment prospects are also limited without a high school credential, and earning a living wage that would allow enough money for housing can be a challenge.

Child welfare caseworkers are required to assist youth ages sixteen and older in foster care to develop independent living plans. Youth are connected to available programs such as the Chafee program or Family Unification Program vouchers (FUPs) that provide financial support for housing. Local programs may help ease the transition from foster care to independent living, but not all young people exiting care access these services. Transitioning to independent living is hard for any young person, and without familial, social, and systemic support, young people exiting foster care are inherently at risk for experiencing homelessness. School stability laws and the national focus on improving educational outcomes for children and youth in foster care are a start, and yet there is still a great deal of work to be done to fully support youth academically and socially.

As we indicated in Chapter 1, there are over 110,000 unaccompanied children and youth experiencing homelessness, some of whom are in foster care. In addition, there are some 23,000 youth who age out of foster care each year (Clemens, Klopfenstein, et al., 2017). Given the statistics cited above, and Blizzard's account of his own experiences, there needs to be substantial revision of our foster care system. More attention needs to be given to identifying those young adults leaving foster care who are likely to experience homelessness, and discharge planning for those young people needs to be substantially improved.

In his implications, Blizzard highlights this need for improvement.

Foster care homes must be operated to mirror normal homes. Cleanliness, dignity, freedom, opportunities, happiness, and stimulation are standard. To prevent ill living quarters and increase social support, diverse groups from the common community, faith based, social workers, teachers, and legislators should physically review foster care homes . . . while including anonymous talks with youth. Youth who wait to enter or leave foster care for various reasons should never be placed in jail, homeless shelters, or unhealthy environments.

He goes on to argue these youth should receive support until the physical age of maturity, twenty-six for females and twenty-eight for males. He concludes,

Generally, youth in foster care are permitted to sign themselves out of care at age eighteen, meaning they can leave a system aimed at supporting them before they could graduate high school, many of whom do so during a bout of a show of independence. Unfortunately, this decision, made at a very young age during a time in which a youth developmentally seeks independence, can have lasting negative consequences as they are generally unable to seek support once they have made the decision to leave the system. Oftentimes, the combination of leaving care, numerous moves, and the chronic instability of placements, leads to significant achievement and learning gaps in students who have entered foster care.

We concur wholeheartedly with these sentiments. There should be a thorough national examination of the age at which foster youth age out of this system. Furthermore, it is essential that organizational bodies that identify and oversee foster care placements spend the time necessary to complete a thorough examination of potential foster parents.

Placements and Diversity

One of the remarkable aspects of Blizzard's account is the diversity of people with whom he interacted, including the three families that he lived with. As he says, "From the tender age of twelve, I was thankfully in systems and other family homes. Native Americans cared for me, such as Ute, Arapahoe, Lakota, and Apache. My cellmates, foster care roommates, homeless homies, and solitary confinement neighbors were Laotians, skinheads, rural mountain Mexicans, inner-city black best friends, hippy kids, CMG Blood, Wigga Crip, and sexually abused teen cowboys." According to Blizzard, his second family was "the United Nations of homes; all races and countries represented—black, Hebrew, Lakota, Peach, Mexican moto gangz, Samoan, Christian."

One gets the distinct impression that Blizzard is very proud of the rich diversity of people with whom he lived and interacted. It is also clear that his three families—a multicultural haven, the UN of homes, and a Mexican family—were instrumental in helping him take charge of his life and engage in a path toward self-sufficiency, long-term employment, marriage, and a family. It is just these kinds of environments that we must create for older youth who have been driven away from families and those who have left an untenable family situation voluntarily. These types of informal kinship situations are a central part of how we can address homelessness more successfully as discussed in the last chapter, and we must be on the constant lookout for such families.

Homelessness and the Criminal Justice System

Blizzard's experience in jail highlights another important aspect of the overall homelessness scenario, namely, the relationship between being without a home and the criminal justice system. As Tobin and Murphy (2016, p. 44) indicated,

> Between 1980 and 2005, the US prison population quadrupled (Pastore & Maguire, 2005), bringing another variable into the homelessness equation. Additionally, the deinstitutionalization movement of the 1960s and 1970s resulted in many mentally ill persons having no shelter, while the concurrent criminalization of mental illness created a situation that leaves mental illness, incarceration, and homelessness hopelessly entangled (McNiel, Binder, & Robinson, 2005). Persons on the streets are at increased risk of being arrested and jailed; conversely, people leaving prison often find themselves with no homes to which they can return (Metraux, Roman, & Cho, 2007). Researchers believe that as many as one in five people who leave prison become homeless; indeed, a California Department of Corrections study found that in San Francisco and Los Angeles, the percentage of parolees who are homeless is between 30 and 50 percent (National Alliance to End Homelessness, 2015).

In many cases, jails have become the country's shelters of last resort for those experiencing homelessness, and, to make matters worse, some of the inmates in our local jails who have no home are there because they do not have the resources to pay for even the most modest fines. In addition, as Tobin and Murphy (2016) suggested, those inmates who do leave are often discharged to the streets. Thus, discharge planning for those released from the criminal justice system must become a major focus if we are to eliminate the revolving door.

A tragic corollary to the revolving door of the criminal justice system for many of those experiencing homelessness is that a common response to people actually living on the streets has been a major effort across the country to criminalize homelessness. The National Law Center on Homelessness and Poverty (2017) recently reported a marked increase in local statutes that negatively affect the lives of people experiencing homelessness in the 187 cities that they surveyed. These ordinances include camping bans, sit and lie ordinances, restrictions on panhandling, antiloitering and vagrancy statutes, and penalties for sleeping in public, and even for living in one's own vehicle. Other local statutes have mushroomed nationwide (National Law Center on Homelessness and Poverty, 2017). Significantly, these statutes tend to target people of color, as they are vastly overrepresented in the population of those without homes (Olivet & Dones, 2018).

Such local efforts to ban certain behaviors and to stigmatize people experiencing homelessness are increasing, despite two crucial factors: enforcement of these laws is expensive, absorbing money that could be better used in other ways; and these laws do nothing to address the underlying issue—the lack of housing and needed services that are so important to ending homelessness. The cost of enforcement is significant; in Colorado, for example, enforcement of local statutes cost just six cities an estimated $5 million over five years (Sturm College of Law, 2016), and a recent update of that report indicated that enforcement efforts in Colorado have increased substantially (Sturm College of Law, 2018).

More importantly, the enactment and enforcement of these laws do nothing to end homelessness. The typical street sweeps simply move people along, or as one organization calls it, "Move Along to Where?" With inadequate housing, shelter facilities, bathroom facilities, employment opportunities, and medical and behavioral health facilities, denizens of the street are simply forced to move along to less conspicuous places. Beckett and Herbert (2009) described it this way:

> Banishment does nothing to resolve any of the underlying conditions that generate social marginality, such as poor employment prospects, inadequate affordable housing, or the challenges of addiction. To the extent that cities increasingly rely on banishment

as a putative solution to disorder, they will succeed only in dis-
placing some individuals from one location to another and in
rendering [their] lives . . . more difficult. (p. 17)

Beckett and Herbert went on to say, "[Banishment] increases the
degree of social marginality experienced by the downtrodden; it
makes their daily struggle for existence more treacherous, their path
to the mainstream more arduous" (2009, p. 22).

In what can only be described as a "politically successful policy
failure" (Beckett & Herbert, 2009, p. 22), the Western Regional
Advocacy Project described the failure this way:

Punitive policies employ the false premise that if you hit a
homeless person hard enough or issue a big enough fine and
then jail them when they don't have the money to pay, then that
person will stop . . . having nowhere to sleep. The fallacy of this
premise is that while the person may leave the park, doorway,
neighborhood, or town, they will still be poor and homeless.
(Quoted in Beckett & Herbert, 2009, p. 25)

There is real irony in the creation of these criminalizing statutes.
Local decisionmakers enact such statutes to eliminate the sometimes
unsightly accumulation of tents and trash and to push unsheltered
individuals into shelters. Local advocates for those experiencing
homelessness respond to these ordinances by initiating demonstra-
tions, lawsuits, and local and state right to rest initiatives. What both
sides of the discussion seem to ignore is the basic fact that both
sides really are after the same goal, namely, getting people off the
streets. Admittedly, each side approaches that goal from a very different perspective. Advocates want a better situation for those on the
streets, including housing and more commodious shelter; they don't
want their folks to have to live the way they do on the streets. Business owners, business improvement districts, business partnerships,
tourists, and often the public want the street people off the streets,
out of their parks, out of sight. In other words, both sides really are
after the same goal. Why is it that the two groups can't collaborate
for the same goal, setting aside their philosophical differences?
Combining the energy and resources of both camps would make the
effort that much stronger.

It is also true that "doing the right thing" (i.e., providing the
unsheltered the kind of housing and services they need) is less expensive than leaving them to incur the costs of both the health-care and

the criminal justice systems. Starting with the seminal study by Culhane, Metraux, and Hadley (2002) and made famous by Gladwell's (2006) *New Yorker* article entitled "Million Dollar Murray," a variety of studies have demonstrated that it costs less to house and provide services for those experiencing chronic homelessness than it does to leave them on the streets to rack up public system expenses, often on a revolving-door basis (see, for example, Hines, 2018).

As Blizzard's story describes so poignantly, there are major issues with our current foster care system and with the way our criminal justice system interacts with homelessness. There are clearly major steps that we as a country must take to improve our foster care system and our criminal justice system as they relate to homelessness, and we must dial back substantially our national drive to criminalize homelessness.

7

Social Networks:
Leanne's Journey

Leanne, a military veteran and a senior staff member in the defense industry, suddenly lost her job and her home during a major economic downturn. Her sixteen months of homelessness provide an opportunity to explore the unfortunate unpredictability of economic crises, like the most recent Great Recession, and their effects, and the importance of networks of friends in times of trouble.

Leanne's Story

Be the Best

I am the quintessential firstborn child of a mother who was raised to be a mother, and a father who had no interest in being a husband, or a parent. My auspicious birth occurred a mere five days before the assassination of Martin Luther King Jr. Coming into my year of jubilee, I own and embrace the combination of chromosomes, ticks, and quirks I inherited from my parents. It has taken nearly all my years to accept the negative characteristics with the same level of enthusiasm and understanding I have for the positive traits. Now that I'm older, and have experienced a life broad, full, and varied, I can point to

specific seasons that served my evolution. Without fear of con-
tradiction, I declare my season of homelessness the single most
life-altering, and life-affirming, event of my life.

It is a common narrative for the firstborn to be the leader of
the pack, reliable, diligent, conscientious, structured, even con-
trolling. Looking back over my formative years, I was all those
things, and more. Each of these serves to achieve the ultimate
state of those who lead the way: be the best at EVERYTHING, or
die trying. Being the best can be both a blessing and a curse.

The Military

By the time I was eleven years old, my younger brother, baby
sister, and I were already latchkey kids. It was my responsibility to make sure they were up, fed, and on their way to school.
My own route home from school included a stop at the elementary school to collect my sister before starting the walk home.
Mom would leave work and make her beeline to us en route,
generally in time to pick us up; often enough, she would pull up
within minutes of my closing the front door.

Age eleven also brought my first serious thoughts about
earning my own money for the things I wanted. My mom gave
me direction that would immediately label me as hardheaded:
Get. A. Job.

There was but one opportunity for employment for a child in
1980, and I could not do it until I turned twelve years old. The
Columbus (Ohio) *Dispatch* needed newspaper carriers, and I was
determined to be the best paper carrier they ever had. I delivered
the evening and weekend edition of the *Columbus Dispatch* for
nearly two years. Like the mail carrier, come rain, sleet, heat of
day, or snow, I walked the block. My papers were folded with
precision, my toss was perfection, and I was never called back
out to replace a paper that was wet or otherwise damaged or
incomplete. At twelve years old, I earned $60 per month, and
with every toss, I felt my liberty swell and take hold of me in a
way that served my ambition and fed my perfectionism.

From the age of twelve until shortly before I entered the US
Air Force, I held many jobs. Although I was not scared of hard
work, nor did I shy away from demonstrating my ambition,
hard work, and conscientiousness, I developed a low tolerance

for injustice or any perceived slight. I was fired from as many jobs as I quit, but I was never without employment, or without the next opportunity in the queue.

I was considered bright and articulate. And by my sophomore year of high school, I was one of thirty-two kids identified to attend a math and science high school for my junior and senior years. The Battelle Memorial Institute, in partnership with the Ohio State University, piloted the Battelle Youth Science Program, a program designed to provide access to the wide world of STEM.

By my junior year, I was carrying a rigorous math and science curriculum, already had three years of French instruction and two years of Spanish instruction, was working part-time, and was dating a football player who started on both the offensive and defensive lines. Everything about my life coming into that year pointed to all the right things happening for me for the rest of my natural life.

After many declarations from my dad about not going into debt to finance my college education, any postsecondary education I chose to do would be my sole responsibility. Having missed a couple of key deadlines for college applications and scholarships—high school love makes for strange and slow decisionmaking—I identified the military and its offer of a GI Bill (and tuition assistance) as my only path forward. On a lovely spring day in April, I made my way to recruitment row. By the afternoon of that lovely spring day in April, I was an air force enlistee, and I would be heading to basic military training in November of that year (1986).

Like many young people who strike out on their own, I made more than my fair share of mistakes and missteps. Fortunately, I had firstborn ways to help me self-correct. And my penchant for leadership and learning didn't go unnoticed by my supervisors and leadership. In retrospect, it was my take-charge ways, ambition, and diligence about being the best at everything that created a way for me, over my mistakes and missteps.

I transitioned into the defense contracting arena with the help and support of a fellow veteran. He and I took college classes together when we were both on active duty, and he had me in mind as he looked to take a promotion with the defense contractor he was working for. My first job was ensuring that all the printers had paper and printer toner and managing the backup and restore system for the software developers and support staff. I would spend the next fifteen years working during the day, furthering my education at night, and pursuing all the interest areas that piqued my curiosity. Having served in the military, I knew how to create a network, let my leadership see my ambition and motivation, and ask for additional responsibilities and new opportunities.

In time, I was serving in executive leadership, being mentored, and offered strategic opportunities by the C-suite (i.e., senior top executives), and traveling the nation over as a representative of a Fortune 500 company. I walked bone straight. I walked with shoulders back. And I walked about the world with my chin up, and thrust out, in full anticipation of a phenomenal future.

Laid Off and Homeless

It would be another several years, and an extended season of joblessness and eventual homelessness, before I understood how closely firstborn tendencies like self-confidence and ambition were linked to outright arrogance. This self-evaluation would not begin until I was laid off a second time in two years, following a tumultuous personal relationship that ran aground, and an eventual season of homelessness.

I was first laid off in February of 2006. It felt like a betrayal. I had no doubt that I would be picked up, and soon. By September 2006, I was picked up by the same corporation but a different business unit, in San Diego, and was appointed the director of performance excellence for the Expeditionary Warfare Center. By the following year, I was recruited to headquarters on the East Coast and back on my A game. Or so I thought.

Like many others during the financial collapse of 2008, leading up to the Romney/Obama election, I was laid off. By then, I was senior management and had been away from my engineering skill set for many years. Although I didn't anticipate the length of time it would take to find employment, I did not doubt that I would. I decided to return to Colorado, where my network remained strong and I was a known entity. My landing back in familiar territory soon revealed that many in my network, and the business we all worked for, had met a similar fate.

From the time I was laid off back East, and for several months after my return, I maintained the lifestyle and mind-set I held dear throughout my career. It would have been prudent for me to scale back, but I didn't. It would have been wise to admit to myself that this layoff season was different than the last; that everyone was struggling; that I needed to transition to a more austere way of living. But, I didn't.

After surrendering my stock options, cashing out my 401K and other investment accounts, and living to the standard at which I had grown accustomed, I lost my safety net and my housing. I would be without my own home for sixteen months. Unlike so many who find themselves experiencing homelessness, I had a very strong network of friends, most of whom I met working in the military or the defense industry. In the beginning, I was able to stay with friends. They were lovely and hospitable. They were patient and kind. But eventually something mysterious happened.

As time churned on, the way I viewed myself began to change. I was less confident and more self-doubting. I stopped eating, and sleep would not come. I didn't recognize myself anymore, and for the first time in my life, I truly did not know what to do next. For the firstborn, and specifically for me as I had always cared for myself, all of this was particularly disheartening, and exceptionally disorienting. I was a shell of my former self and I was heartbroken.

By the time I found work in March 2010, I had been without a home for sixteen months. A friend and former colleague would be transitioning back East with her husband, who was not able to find work in the Denver metro area but had secured an opportunity in the DC metro area. At the time, I had been living at an Extended Stay, after being asked to leave a friend's home without much warning. I was grateful to be "housesitting" as I was coming perilously close to needing to exit the hotel, because I had no money to stay. I was also hesitant to say yes.

After staying with two girlfriends (and their families), women I thought I knew well, and I thought knew me well, I was asked to leave. And I was asked to leave without any prospects for work or a place to stay. In the first instance, I exited to a battered women's shelter, as a veteran bed was available and "reserved" for me.

My hesitance to say yes to my third girlfriend gave me pause. For the first time, I questioned how I presented for myself.

I still see myself as ambitious, working hard to get my life sorted out, still rocking all my firstborn characteristics. But what if I was mistaken about that? Had I been fooling myself? Had the first two women, both of whom knew me when I was working in the aerospace industry, seen something different? How did I present for them now that I had been unemployed, homeless, but not broken? Was I broken and didn't know that I was showing "broken tendencies"?

It was an awkward conversation, as I recall. Clearly, there had been some communication between her and my first girlfriend, not surprising as we all met working on a military installation and knew one another well. Their conversation served our conversation well. It was revealed that there had been an unmet expectation. While I was yet unmoored and disoriented by what my life had become, my girlfriend had an expectation that I would be more integrated in her life and the comings and goings of the day-to-day happenings in the household. I never thought that would be the case, at all. In retrospect, I should have suspected it, as I do recall certain disappointed expressions, and statements grounded in frustration, when I declined to participate in certain activities.

The threat of losing a third friendship over my having lost my job, and being unable to find another one, was not a thought I relished. To lose that friendship over unmet, or undercommunicated expectations, would be unbearable. The first two relationships faltered in ways that we still haven't recovered from. Early on, I was consumed by getting my life back on track and worked to stay focused and not ruminate on all that was not going my way. But, when I finally sat with what occurred with these friendships, I mourned their loss and I allowed for grief. I still grieve.

But now, I'd had an opportunity to move into a home setting, where I would be alone often. And when I wasn't alone, my girlfriend would be tending to her small business, her network, and her full life. We were very similar, she and I, so it seemed like it could go all right. I was staying with this friend when the new job opportunity happened.

Although I cannot assert with any certainty that my self-perception was the catalyst for anyone else to see me differently, it was evident I was presenting differently for my friends as well. Even though I was actively looking for employment, I couldn't get an interview. Soon, the queries about "taking anything" came ("What's wrong with working at Walgreens?" "Are you *really* trying?"), as did the eventual question about my time line for moving out. No job. No place to go. In one case it was imperative for my friend to have her "house back," and I suppose that it was something I did understand. I had not expected this season to be this ongoing, either.

There would be months of flopping from pillar to post, couch surfing, and stints at the Extended Stay. I even had my assigned bed at a women's shelter. My household goods were in storage, and for the first time, I was living out of suitcases. It was then that I recalled my leadership on a street ministry. I had some cursory knowledge about the compassion industry from that experience, and at the time spent significant time learning about the domain. Skill sets I honed during my career had been useful during that season of learning, and it was becoming apparent that I would likely need some of the services I learned about. I set about reacquainting myself with the compassion industry. I had been reintroduced to faith following a rollover accident in April 2000. By 2002, I was leading the street ministry for a Missionary Baptist Church in Aurora.

Given the length and terms of my homelessness (at least some of the time, I was couch surfing), I was certain that I would not qualify as "chronically" homeless. With a full understanding that those administering the grants would want to demonstrate success and would be motivated by my candidacy in their program, I was confident that I would at least qualify for housing and job training assistance, although I wouldn't likely qualify for wraparound services. Or, at least, that was my thinking.

In the case of homelessness, its own broad and vast problem to solve, there are customer requirements that the solution must encompass, measured in specific outcomes, and a budget. However, unlike the defense contractor, most nonprofit agencies lack the capacity to staff full teams. They are largely reliant on a single grant writer, whose cut-and-paste skills surpass those of the average human being.

The compassion industry requires the opposite of who I presented myself to be. Money only flowed to these agencies when men and women had criminal histories, drug or alcohol addictions, minor children, no income to speak of, and no transportation. After making countless telephone calls, and filling out even more applications, it became clear that I would not be the ideal candidate for the compassion industry. Not without lying about my status. And in at least one case, that's precisely what I was "asked" to do.

New Job, New Home

A colleague from moons ago reached out to me to inquire about my work status, as she heard that I had been laid off, and things were not going very well. She, an air force veteran, knew a marine veteran who was starting her own staffing business, and she thought I would be an ideal candidate for a new contract that was recently awarded to the company I used to work for.

My ability to remember the dates of significant events borders on the savant. On March 19, I interviewed with the hiring manager for what would be a contract job, on a new software development. I would be responsible for a $60 million bill of materials procurement and overall systems engineering support. It was a perfect fit, and I was interviewing on my brother's birthday, so it felt like kismet. I received the call I hoped for, the same afternoon, and I would start my new job on March 30th, my birthday, at $71 per hour.

I took the offer letter as proof of employment to an apartment complex not far from my friend's house. I arranged to move in on April 8th, and I was ecstatic! At lease up, I had not had a mortgage, a lease, or utilities in my own name for sixteen months. I had an address at the UPS Store in the Denver metro area, a box I secured when I took the job in San Diego, but no real bills to pay. I was perplexed by how much I had gotten out of the habit of doing for myself or tending to a household. I immediately traded my hooptie for a brand-new car, using the same offer letter, and then set about buying myself a new wardrobe for work. I'd lost a lot of weight during the sixteen months, much of it I didn't notice at first, and what I had no longer fit. There were pieces, mainly blazers, pant suits, and skirt suits that I wanted to keep, so I had them altered. But, I also went all in on handbags, new shoes, and accessories.

Righting the train again became frenzied and elating. I started to buy at a dizzying pace. I denied myself very little that I wanted, feeling justified and needy. Soon, although I would not know it for some time, I was harboring fear and resentment. I feared all of it going away and finding myself in the precise predicament I was in before this opportunity came along. Now that I was back in the right context, that is to say, I was "balling" again, I was back on the A list. My phone was ringing again. I was invited to lunch, dinner, and the occasional happy hour. I was back on the list for the Pampered Chef, candle, and jewelry parties. It was just like the previous sixteen months, and the personal and emotional trauma it brought, had not occurred at all.

However, I was angry. That anger manifested in strange ways. Eventually, I had the wherewithal to see this about myself. As is the case with trauma, we can pull a thread directly back to childhood. It was no different with me. I had gone from being the overachieving firstborn child, with most everything I touched turning to my advantage somehow, to not being able to do that. At all. For months. And during that season, with one noted exception, those I held in the highest regard, and who I thought held me the same way, could not wait for me to leave their homes. All of them knew me when I led homeless ministry for my church, several years before. None of them concerned themselves with where I would end up, only that I was, in fact, going.

There is a common question asked of men and women who find themselves unhoused. I've asked it myself: "Why can't you stay with family or friends?" With the question comes a presumption: they must have *done* something not to be welcome with family or friends. They must have, right? How else does a family member, or friend, turn you down—or out—given the predicament you are in? It MUST be their fault.

I no longer ask that question. Nor do I make presumptions about what could have gone wrong or assign fault. I've only my own story to refer to. Regardless, the sentiment was so ingrained in the fibers of my being, going home was not even on my list of options when I found myself needing a home to go to. My parents are yet unaware of that leg of my journey, as I never presented the circumstances as dire as they were, nor did I ask for any financial support. In truth, my parents are not well off. And I was confident that I would be back on track long before I was.

Losing friendships that fall into the lifetime category was especially hurtful, and more than a little disorienting. As I am aware of this dynamic, when everyone involved is presumably "normal," how much more difficult is it for the men and women who are dealing with addictions, mental illness, and trauma, to maintain friendships, or keep their networks intact? It's exceptionally more difficult, and that's why I no longer ask the question.

I also don't judge someone for making the decisions they make with whatever money befalls them. There was a time that I would have judged me harshly for all the spending I did soon after my employment in 2010. How dare I spend what I want, when I want, on what I want, when only weeks before, I was relying on the kindness of someone else? Hell, wisdom should tell me to save for that rainy day, right? But it turns out that I did not fundamentally change. I had been earning money since I turned twelve years old and had only found myself with an opportunity for the long-term once. That one time was a doozy, but it was only one time.

As I ponder this notion called resilience, there's one thing I am certain of. I spent plenty of time during the sixteen months feeling like I had been dethroned. I occurred for myself as the Queen of Damn Near Everything. There is nothing more disorienting than every one of your "superpowers" being neutralized, when you're accustomed to the shock and awe of your own strength and being able to summon it whenever you need to.

Although disoriented, I was determined to keep going. Without question, there were days that I did not want to get out of a bed that wasn't mine, fluff up, put my game face on, and get out into the mean streets. There weren't many, but there were a few. And, on the most severe of those days, I did not. The good news is that I didn't allow for two such days to string together. After all, the quintessential firstborn child cannot be off her game for two days in a row.

My life until now, from the first job, those fateful sixteen months, and whatever comes next, serves my continued work in this space. I had not imagined a life where an air force veteran, with a software engineering degree, and such a varied set of experiences and opportunities, would land squarely in the compassion space, prepared for the work.

Yet, here I am, having the time of my life.

Implications

Veteran Homelessness

One of Leanne's important characteristics is that she, like Michelle in the next story, was an African American veteran, part of the significant subpopulation among those experiencing homelessness. There seems to be a national sentiment that homeless veterans deserve our assistance, perhaps more than any other subpopulation, because of their service to our country. Ever since the days of the Vietnam veteran returnees, the closure of VA psychiatric facilities in the 1970s, and the more recent influx of returnees from the Gulf War, Iraq, and Afghanistan, there has been considerable interest in doing what we can for these "deserving" individuals. The data clearly suggest something does need to be done.

As of December 2017, according to HUD's Annual Homelessness Assessment Report (AHAR) to Congress, 40,056 veterans were experiencing homelessness, 9.1 percent of the total homeless population in January of that year. Of these veterans, 62 percent were staying in shelters or transitional housing programs, and the remaining 15,366 veterans were sleeping in places that were not suitable for human habitation.

Although these numbers may seem high, what is particularly striking is the progress we have made nationally in addressing veteran homelessness. Between 2009, when the annual Point-in-Time survey started identifying veterans specifically, and 2017, there has been a 45 percent decrease in veteran homelessness. During this same period, the number of unsheltered vets declined by 49 percent, and the sheltered vet numbers decreased by 43 percent (US Department of Housing and Urban Development, 2017a).

During this time period, there was a major commitment at the federal level to provide the resources necessary to address veteran homelessness. The Obama White House and the Department of Veterans Affairs poured substantially greater resources into the effort, and the VA administrator, Shaun Donovan, made it a priority to significantly reduce veteran homelessness.

The success of this effort, both nationally and in some states and cities across the country, provides real hope about our ability to address homelessness. If the political will is there, at the top and in states and local jurisdictions, and if elected officials then provide the resources and oversight to maximize the implementation of these reduction efforts, we have demonstrated that we can have a major impact on reducing homelessness. However, the lesson is clear: There must be strong political will pushing this, and that has to translate into significantly increased resources. Nothing short of that will suffice.

Economic Downturns

Given the history of the US economy over the past 250 years, it is clear that unexpected glitches in the system can produce disastrous consequences. This history is riddled with peaks and valleys, times of boom and great expansion and times of recession, even economic depression as we experienced in the late 1920s and 1930s. Such was the case in the period between 2008 and 2010, as the banking industry helped to fuel a host of "underwater" mortgages and the resulting housing foreclosures. Just as important, this Great Recession forced many corporations to cut back their operations by, in part, laying off staff. Leanne was caught in this economic vise, suffering a layoff that led to homelessness.

Currently, the US economy is humming along, with lower unemployment, growing consumer satisfaction, a galloping stock market, and tight lids on inflation. However, there are potential signs on the horizon that could signal another downturn. Trade tariffs and resulting trade wars could bring higher consumer costs. Due to improving technology, some jobs, especially those at the lower end of the employment ladder, may disappear, leaving many employees without jobs, as Andrew Yang (2018) argued in his book, *The War on Normal People: The Truth About America's Disappearing Jobs and Why Universal Basic Income Is Our Future*. Wind, solar, and nuclear energy are slowly replacing the more traditional sources, thus creating the possibility of more displaced workers in the coal industry.

As we face a new cohort of unemployed and underemployed workers, we must create new types of jobs. For example, online retail purchasing is expanding rapidly, thus creating new opportunities. However, even here, individuals need to obtain certifications in the field of technology as we do not have enough skilled workers to fill these high-paying positions, which generally do not require a college degree. Another arena for job growth stems from the desperate need for increased attention to our national infrastructure. Roads, highways, bridges, water systems, sewer systems are often forty, fifty, sixty years old or even older and badly in need of repair. A massive effort to attend to this need, not unlike several of the programs of the New Deal, would be a significant deterrent to the possibility of increasing unemployment.

Furthermore, wages across the board have stagnated. As Bristow Hardin (2016) pointed out, between 1979 and 2013, wages for workers at the tenth percentile fell by 5.3 percent. In addition, in the roughly thirty years from 1979 to 2007, after-tax income for people in the lowest quintile of income earners grew by only 18 percent, not even keeping up with cost of living increases. The federal minimum wage of $7.25 has not changed since 2009, and it has increased only slightly since 1981, although individual states have the authority to increase the minimum wage above the federal minimum in their own jurisdictions. For example, the current minimum wage in Colorado, our home state, is $11.10, but that is almost $15 per hour less than the housing wage, what an individual needs to earn to afford an average two-bedroom residence in Denver.

As Tobin and Murphy (2016) pointed out, "More recent reports have suggested that employment among people experiencing homelessness may be around 45%. We should be clear, however, that many of the people without housing are unemployed, many chronically so, and most of the individuals who do have jobs are underemployed or work on the bottom rungs of the labor market ladder" (p. 35). To address this untenable situation will require an increase in minimum wages across the country and a marked improvement in our ability to develop workforce opportunities. It is unacceptable that a person working full-time anywhere cannot afford housing.

A recent report by Bivens and Shierholz (2018) indicated that wage growth in the United States between the 1970s and 2016 has fallen way behind worker productivity, thus further increasing economic inequality between the top 10 percent of workers and the bottom 90 percent. One of the factors that they identify for this divergence is the weakened power of the workforce, and they recommend that policies be enacted that would permit greater unionization of workers, particularly lower-wage ones. If we are to see improved wages and working conditions (including company-provided health care) such that wages provide enough income to enable true self-sufficiency, then improving workers' ability to persuade employers to provide this seems highly desirable.

Not surprisingly, the issue of maintaining a permanent home is directly tied to the ability to earn an income, and income growth over time. While productivity in the United States has risen by over 73 percent since 1973, hourly pay has increased a mere 12.5 percent, meaning productivity outpaced wage growth nearly six times over between 1973 and 2016 (Economic Policy Institute, 2017). In terms of wage growth between 1979 and 2017, wage earners under the median income only saw a 10 percent increase, while those at or above the 90th percentile saw a 40 percent increase (Gordon, 2018).

Falling wages are in spite of increased educational attainment. Low-wage workers, or those in the bottom 20 percent of income earners, obtain high school degrees at a rate of 78 percent and college educations at 44 percent, yet their wages continue to decline (Hardin, 2016). With these increased levels of education also come the high cost and long-term debt of obtaining these degrees. According to a national analysis completed by the Institute for College Access and Success (2018), the average college graduate in 2017 had $28,650 in student loan debt, a number that continues to increase over time. The report pointed out that a disproportionate number of students from low-income families, first-generation college students, and students of color are borrowers, increasing the rate of eventual default by these groups.

The wage disparity and debt burden contribute to the growing imbalance in the distribution of wealth. As Hardin (2016) described, regarding data collected in 2010, "of every 100 people, the richest person owned 42 percent of all financial wealth in 2010; the next richest 19 people owned 54 percent; and the remaining 80 people held a meager 5 percent" (p. 184). The American Dream is dying a slow, economic death as income distribution continues to move disproportionately toward the wealthiest individuals in our country.

In light of these data, it is imperative that we establish a much higher minimum wage on the national level. Such an increase will have major implications for people in poverty and will help large numbers of those experiencing homelessness afford housing.

Another significant implication of Leanne's story is the need to focus more attention on prevention. For someone like Leanne, unemployment insurance was one safeguard, but the current system of such insurance is inadequate. Twenty-six weeks of reimbursement was less than half the time that she was unemployed and housing unstable. We need to develop longer periods of benefits for those who are laid off from work.

For those at the bottom of the economic ladder, it is imperative that we have a greater understanding of the financial resources that people need, a better grasp of who among the extremely poor is likely to move into homelessness, and a greater appreciation for how long it may be necessary to provide some level of financial support to those in severe economic hardship. As we pointed out in Chapter 1, we have not figured out how to prevent significant numbers of people from becoming homeless over the last forty years; this must become a much higher priority at all levels of the public and private sectors.

Support Networks

Leanne's support networks proved to be a mixed bag. Three of her friends and colleagues provided temporary housing during her period of homelessness, but each made it clear that this was very temporary. Close friends and supporters became occasional acquaintances at best. Leanne expresses real dismay and sadness about the disintegration of these relationships and the impact that has had on her life.

One of the characteristics of homelessness that often goes unrecognized is the shame of the person experiencing it. As Leanne indicates in her story, her "friends" kept asking her, "Why don't you ask your family for help?" Part of the answer was her sense of shame about being in that situation. Another part was her clear understanding of her parents' economic situation and not wanting to be a financial burden on them. Homelessness creates real psychological trauma, and all of those in helping situations must recognize that and proceed with trauma-informed practices.

On the other hand, another of her natural supporters was solely responsible for reaching out to Leanne and alerting her to a perfect job opening, thus ending her period of being without a home of her own. From this standpoint, her network of supporters was crucial for her escaping homelessness. One lesson to be learned from Leanne's story is the importance of maintaining these networks of support. The care and feeding of these networks are paramount, even though it may be very difficult in times of great stress. In many cases, homelessness may be the result of, or worsened by, a lack of network. For example, Green, Tucker, Golinelli, and Wenzel (2013) found that chronically homeless men in Los Angeles had significantly higher rates of fragmented social networks than men experiencing episodic homelessness. Groton and Radey's (2018) study concluded that unaccompanied women experiencing homelessness identified a loss of support networks, most commonly the death of a family member or the exhaustion of their network, as a direct pathway into homelessness. Thus, service agency personnel need to be alert to an individual's networks and be aware of ways to aid in the maintenance of them. Furthermore, if such networks do not actually exist for an individual experiencing homelessness, service agencies really need to help initiate and develop them at the outset.

It is also true that Leanne found considerable support in her faith community and in what she calls "the compassion industry." Her engagement with her church and with faith-based efforts to address homelessness and poverty provided a real anchor for her during her months of homelessness. Although we are not recommending that every individual experiencing homelessness become a member of a faith community, we are suggesting that faith communities can become an important source of support for people struggling with homelessness. In Colorado, for example, the statewide program, One Congregation, One Family, in which individual congregations create mentor/support teams to assist families and seniors who are experiencing homelessness, has provided assistance to over 1,000 families over the past several years (Denver Leadership Foundation, n.d.).

We must be ever vigilant regarding support networks and community. Whether it's incentivizing individuals to provide a caring and helping hand or developing strategies to form helping networks of support, it is imperative that we figure out ways to provide support for those experiencing homelessness.

8

Client-Centered Solutions: Michelle's Journey

The experience of a second African American veteran provides another opportunity to explore racial bias, the sense that people of a different race are either the enemy or invisible, in our society. The administrative/accounting error that forced Michelle into homelessness and had such a profound effect on her life demonstrates the potential danger that many of us face—how just one mistake, not of our own doing, can ruin our lives. On a more positive note, her network helped her get through this frightening experience, despite the shame and the cookie-cutter manner in which her situation was addressed.

Michelle's Story

Am I Invisible?

I am a black woman; how could I be invisible? It is a tale to tell, all part of my tale of what I will call my two years at the spa (two years of being homeless). I kept the fact that I became homeless from my mother, father, children, some of my closest friends, and most people that knew me because I felt ashamed. In doing this,

I was privy to the thoughts and attitudes of many of those around me regarding those that were homeless or living in poverty.

I want to tell you a little of what it was like through my eyes, a veteran, a black woman, a person with a career and a degree, a volunteer in the community, a mentor, and a leader who lost her home and became homeless, a person without a roof. I was the person that people used to count on for help, the one that took people in, served those experiencing homelessness and then, almost in the blink of an eye, I lost my home. I never thought I was immune to becoming homeless; I just never thought about becoming homeless because I was always working and doing for others. I was too busy to become homeless; God needed me to keep taking care of others.

My Adventure

In 2011, I was living in Houston, working as a paralegal part-time, going to night school at the University of Houston full-time, and teaching a legal secretary program at a technical college during the day. During the fall of 2011, my job ended, and I decided I could finally do something for myself since my three children were adults and my twenty-eight-year marriage had ended. I thought about moving to Chicago, New York, or Colorado to finish my degree. I was accepted at the University of Colorado at Denver on the Auraria Campus (UCD), so I was moving to Denver. I had money in the bank, investments, an apartment, my severance, qualification for financial aid, excellent letters of reference, a paralegal degree, experience; I had everything I needed to make a successful move.

On December 19, I arrived in Castle Rock, Colorado, after a long drive. I settled into my apartment, and on Christmas Day I delivered meals for Meals on Wheels in Denver. It was my first time driving in snow and ice; it was a treacherous adventure but very satisfying.

After the holidays, I went to register for school, but due to a glitch at UCD, I was not allowed to begin school in the spring of 2012 as planned; therefore, I was not able to get the financial aid that I had calculated into my budget to supplement my income. I applied for unemployment, which was granted, so I did have some income. I began searching for a job until I could begin school.

My Homelessness

However, work was not coming, and was I getting nervous! I was applying everywhere. I learned that there were no jobs in Castle Rock. I started looking north to Denver, thinking that with my experience, I would be a good catch. WRONG! Some employers thought I was overqualified and that I would not stay, and some thought I was of the wrong aesthetic. My depression began to set in when I could not find a job, and my bank account withered. During the previous few months, I had not spent all my money, including my investments; by investments, I mean the small amount of money that I had put into an IRA, which totaled less than $7,000. So, I made my mind up to give up my apartment, liquidate my investments, put my furniture in storage, and move into a shelter where there were other female veterans. My therapist helped me to locate a place that was near the university and close to a secure storage facility. The shelter had a large room downstairs where only female vets stayed. It had a nice bathroom and six beds. It was very clean, but I was scared and there was no room for my *stuff*. I need to be near my stuff, and of course, I have that PTSD thing.

The so-called intake was a joke, but I had to keep in mind that I didn't want my car to be my zip code, plus I was so tired from moving out of my apartment and getting my furniture into the storage unit that I was not thinking very clearly. It had been a very long day. The first night, I just passed out from exhaustion. In the next day or so, I had the option to move to a small hotel next to the shelter; I refer to it as the lovely Hanoi Hilton. I would have a room of my own with a kitchenette (small hotel room). They made all kinds of assurances—no single males, no loitering, and safety. Ha ha!! I moved in, got some of my stuff from storage, took a bath, bought some fresh food for the fridge, and some sheets. I started to breathe, but they were short breaths. I still hadn't told anyone that I was homeless. I told my family that I was living in a dorm with female vets. At the Hanoi Hilton, I was really beginning to understand the art of being homeless. I made the room look and feel as nice as I could; I was determined to make the best of it. I bought some dishes, rabbit ears for the TV, towels, soaps, groceries, and a candle. Yes, I spent some of the money from my unemployment check; just because I was homeless didn't mean that I had lost my desire for nice things. I just purchased them at the Dollar Store and Walmart instead of the usual places. I would make believe it was better.

After the holidays, I was very busy getting registered at school. I took a full load of classes and got acquainted with the Vet Student Center on campus. I would come to find that the Vet Center on campus would be my lifeline. It was at the Vet Center that I would meet Cameron, my marine. I felt he was one of two personal angels that God put in my path to help me with the fire that I would encounter at school. Every time there was a roadblock at school, Cameron would help me hurdle it and sometimes crawl under it; once or twice we even busted right through it, carrying the banner Fuck You. You see, Cameron is a man of ethics and equity for everyone, not just sometimes but all of the time. Like me, he believes what is right is right and we should always do the right thing at all costs no matter how much money we make or how many times we fall down.

Person-Centered Services?

At the Hanoi Hilton, I was assigned other case managers from the VA since I am a veteran. Meetings, meetings, meetings became the rule of the day. The goal was to document numbers to turn in to the VA. I told the case managers, I have a plan: finish my degree, get a job, and get on with my life. They had one thought: everyone who was without a home/roof was an addict, alcoholic, could not manage their money, and had no discipline. "Well," I told them, "I don't abuse alcohol, use or abuse legal or illegal drugs. I have raised three children; they have all gone to college; and I have earned one degree and am working on a second. I took the USAF to court and won my case. I handled my own divorce case, and you say that I need to go to life management classes?" I was mandated to attend all of these meetings and actually leave class to attend meetings that have nothing to do with me just so "they can have numbers to turn in." I already attended therapy at the Vet Center; I was doing that before I left Texas and had that in place when I arrived in Colorado. I found myself getting very frustrated with case managers who thought the process was more important than the individual. Not all people are the same, so the case managers cannot and should not attempt to apply all of the same variables to everyone.

There is something about the nature of a system of the people saying they are there to help you and yet they are the very ones causing you agony. How can they help you when they never ask what it is that you need? Cameron and I discussed my being homeless and the case managers' wanting me to leave class to come to meetings that had nothing to do with me. I could not get them to understand that I only needed shelter until I completed my education and that none of my behavior caused me to lose my home. My leaving class or the campus would have been detrimental to doing my best in school; I thought understanding that was not rocket science. I was told by the case managers that if I did not comply with the meetings, I would lose my shelter. I asked them, "Just to be clear, if I don't leave school to attend meetings that have nothing to do with me, you would take my shelter away?" They would never say yes; they would always say, "If you do not comply with the meetings, you will have to leave the program." Same thing, right?

When I told Cameron all of this, he decided to go with me to the meeting; of course, I did not tell them he was coming. Imagine the look on their faces when he walked in. He said the very same thing I said; he and I made sure of that, but, oh my gosh, the response was totally different when a white male approached the situation. Not only did I not have to attend the meetings, but if they needed me, they would come to his office on the school campus when I was not in class; WTF, the power of a white male never ends, even if it is used for a black homeless female. I pimped him out to get what I needed. You see, they never heard me when I said the very same thing; I was invisible and voiceless because if you are roofless, you have no choice, no sense, and no value. Like I said, I am black; how can I be invisible? Because I had no internet at the Hanoi Hilton, Cameron arranged for me to have a key to the Student Vet Center on campus so that I could do my homework. I lived there virtually from the time the school was open at 6:30 a.m. until after midnight.

New Opportunities and Bumps on the Path

My HIV volunteer work led me to attend Colorado Organizations Responding to AIDS meetings. There I met Jeff Thormodsgaard, a lobbyist. He introduced me to the capitol and the business of getting things done. Everything moved at the speed of sound; my three-inch heels needed wheels. Jeffrey had opened the door to a new world for me and I liked it; box it up for me. Through Jeffrey, I met Representative Rhonda Fields, and I liked her straightaway. I spent time with her in the chamber and in her office. We would go to events on the weekends, and before long, I became her aide.

Things at the Hanoi Hilton remained miserable; critters in and out of my room, destroying my possessions. I was in fear every day. My life was miserable every day. One of the worst times was the hotel office sending the police that hunt missing felons who have open warrants up to my room in the middle of the night looking for someone.

Too many things, too much, too much. I was waking up every day wondering what it was going to be today. I was so tired of being bullied by them and of their talking out of the other side of their mouths, saying they were here to help me. In the meeting with the shelter/Hanoi Hilton, I do remember telling them that all they had done for me was give me a roof over my head, and it was not a safe one. Oopsy. After that comment, I was told I was out; thirty days and I was to vacate my room, right in the middle of finals. November 19 would be my last day at the Hanoi Hilton.

I had another lifeline at school in the Vet Center and that was Izzy (army); he was my Boots to Suits sponsor and adviser. (Boots to Suits is a group for juniors and seniors who are veterans; they can be assigned mentors and internships in their chosen field of study.) Izzy was there for me when Cameron was busy or not available and I needed to vent or needed a shoulder or to just talk. He also connected me to the VFW Post. Izzy got busy helping locate a place for me to live.

January came, and Izzy was still making things happen. I had very good grades and I was in Boots to Suits so Izzy asked if I would like to interview to work as an intern in the governor's office in February of 2014; of course, I said, "okie dokie." I had had such a great time with Representative Fields the year before and I had met so many great people, I could not wait to get back to the Capitol. I had the interview and it was great; I was in and I started right away. Did I mention that this was a paid internship? Having a salary qualified me for a program that helped veterans get housing. I found an apartment that was perfect for me, in the perfect location, and it was safe. I am actually still there.

I left the governor's office to go to work for Dr. Don W. Burnes at the Burnes Institute. I thought this would be the last job of my life, doing work to help service organizations serve people better. I was able to assist Don in teaching a class on homelessness at the University of Denver in the spring of 2014, and it was wonderful. The students all knew I had spent time at the spa, and I was very honest with them about my experiences. I believe it was a positive experience for all of us. Business at the institute was okay but not thriving; agencies wanted evaluations but no one had the money to pay for them. There were no big contracts coming our way, and I was beginning to panic because I just couldn't lose this job and become homeless again. Old thoughts began to creep into my mind, my sleep began to get worse; I was scared but I tried to hide it. I always tried to keep my faith. I always felt that God would never let me down and believed what Joyce Meyer taught me in her preaching, that I could do things while I was afraid. It was awful the day Don called Rhiannon and me into his office to inform us that the end of February would be our last day if a miracle did not happen; I still thought someone would learn to eat paper and shit money to save us. I think this was one of the roughest days of Don's professional career.

Now, back to losing my job; the end of February came, and it was so difficult. February 2014 was the month that I moved into an apartment, and February 2015 was the month that I was afraid of losing it. You know, I feel that I do so much stuff for everyone, when am I going to be able to relax and just live without worry? I have been doing public service since I was seventeen years old; I dragged my kids with me to do for others. I received a public service award during the time that I was homeless, and I have learned to appreciate even the bad shit. I don't want much, just a small house that I can own, a small yard for Edgar (my service dog), a car that is dependable, my health, and a job doing service (that pays). I do know how lucky I am to have a family that loves me so very much, friends that love me, and I survived being homeless and I look at it as a blessing. I do know so many people are doing so much worse; I do live in gratitude every day. I am just venting. It will pass.

I Don't Fit the Stereotype

Let us segue to the present. I am still in my apartment and working full-time. My hope has always been to attend graduate school, but I can't eat paper and shit money. I am the advocacy coordinator for Colorado Cross Disability Coalition, which allows me to work with some of the populations that are most at risk. Many of these people are now or have been homeless. I am often told by those that I serve that they feel I really understand what they are feeling and going through; I attribute this to the gift of having been without a roof.

The most important part of my chapter comes now. I became homeless through no fault of my own, and that should not even matter. I made my move to Colorado with investments, savings, and a plan, all of the things Suzy Orman says you should have. I even had a paralegal degree under my belt, excellent letters of reference, and years of good experience. All of the things that kept me from gaining employment were beyond my control. I have no drug use, no alcohol abuse. I had never missed a day of work due to my PTSD. My mental health issue returned due to becoming homeless and was exacerbated by the case managers and the system that insisted that they were here to help me but only hindered me, trying and almost succeeding in breaking my spirit. I still never used drugs or alcohol. When I didn't fit the stereotype that case managers thought I should fit, they did not know what to do, and it usually resulted in them being angry, and they would check the noncompliance box. I found that with case managers, the process became more important than the individual. The need to increase numbers was the name of the game, hence the response, "This is what the program requires."

I thought that if a service organization's numbers were to decrease and fewer people were coming through their doors, especially repeat clients, that meant their programs were working the best because people were becoming and staying self-sustainable. Therefore, the lower the numbers, the higher the reward, to increase funds to the programs that are working the best. RIGHT.

Homelessness is something that is still difficult for me to say. It has changed me. It still frightens me; I am still afraid to spend any money or relax. It is funny that I am so hard on myself, but I never feel this way about others that have lost their roof.

I wonder if this attitude will ever leave me. It is a heavy bur-den—being a black woman with a disability, a service dog, and being post-homeless. I personally believe that when people make mistakes, it proves they are trying. I wish everyone felt that way. The reason I worry about what others think of me is that it seems that people often don't tend to hear what I say or ask because they are thinking of me and my background.

In summary, I guess I want people to know that the emo-tional effects of homelessness stay with you, just like those of abuse. Getting housing does not fix it, getting a job does not fix it, and having wonderful friends and loved ones doesn't fix it. I thank God for the strength that I found to keep going; I can never ignore the reality of those less fortunate because this is who I am. I believe I had to experience homelessness to be a better advocate for the homeless and people living in poverty.

Implications

Michelle's story should be a wake-up call for all of us because it highlights a number of important issues. Perhaps most important, here is an African American grandmother, a veteran with PTSD, who doesn't smoke, drink to excess, or use drugs; she is a person with a very respectable resume and job, and one who decided to venture forth to further her education. Yet, through an administrative error and absolutely no fault of her own, she was forced into homeless-ness. Her story also illustrates some of the racial inequities in our system, and her treatment while in a shelter—by case managers who failed to listen to her story—borders on frightening.

Totally Unexpected

If there was anyone least likely to end up experiencing homelessness, it was Michelle. After completing a successful military career, she had become a fixture in her hometown of Houston, teaching, being a paralegal, and parenting three successful children who provided her with several grandchildren. Then, because funding ended for her employment situation, she decided to further her education, and she chose to move to Denver to enroll at UCD in part because of a good financial aid package. Furthermore, she had savings and health care, so she assumed the best.

This type of situation can happen to almost anyone, especially if the person experiences a major upheaval in their lives, such as moving to a new town where they know no one. As we saw in the recent Great Recession, home foreclosures and job layoffs can become much more prevalent. Natural disasters are always with us, as is the potential for a medical catastrophe. Family breakups and domestic abuse and violence are not uncommon. Existing wage structures are insufficient at times to ward off homelessness. In short, there are a number of possible causes of losing one's home. The old adage, you are only one paycheck away from homelessness, may be a bit of a stretch, but it's not far off.

Bandwidth

In their book, *Scarcity: The New Science of Having Less and How It Defines Our Lives,* the authors argued that persons who are confronted by a scarcity of resources (e.g., money, food, companionship) often find themselves with what the authors called reduced "bandwidth," and this makes them less insightful, less forward-thinking, less in control (Mullainathan & Shafir, 2013). This is not to suggest that Michelle had less bandwidth. In fact, she had made elaborate plans for her move and matriculation at UCD. Even when she discovered that her aid package would not be forthcoming, she calculated the pros and cons of how best to adjust to her financial situation.

However, it is true that people in extreme poverty and those experiencing homelessness are confronted by scarcity. Because of the daily challenges and bandwidth required for existing and dealing with scarcity, they may be less physically and psychologically able, as Mullainathan and Shafir (2013) argued, to make wise decisions regarding their future. This has important implications for how the homelessness industry provides service to those who are homeless. It becomes important to begin by reducing client stress as much as possible before asking them to make major decisions.

One of the important program efforts that has evolved over the past twenty years to reduce client stress as a precursor to addressing other issues is housing first. Housing first, or the philosophy that individuals should first be placed in housing before trying to deal with other issues that the individual may have, as discussed in Marie's chapter, requires a shift in beliefs. Unlike earlier concepts, such as the Continuum of Care that envisioned a person moving in a step-by-step progression through the homelessness experience and not moving into permanent housing until other issues had been addressed, the basic notion of housing first is that an individual must first be in a stable housing environment before he or she is able to focus on other issues.

The use of the housing first model is how Utah, a traditionally conservative state, has essentially ended chronic homelessness. The state embraced the idea of housing first, recognizing the difficulty in obtaining employment (it is hard to find a job without an address), addressing mental health or substance use disorders, or consistently accessing other supports while living without a home. If an individual has a safe, stable place to sleep each night, they can then focus on some of the underlying causes of their homelessness. Not only is this approach more humane, literally fewer people die in the streets, it is more fiscally responsible. For example, the state of Utah saves approximately $8,000 annually for each person they have successfully gotten off the streets and into housing. Prior to obtaining housing, these individuals were accessing shelters frequently, spending more time in jail, and ending up hospitalized more often, creating a huge strain on these costly systems, a cost the state estimated at $20,000 annually per individual (McCoy, 2015).

Need for Trauma-Informed, Client-Centered Services

Michelle's experiences while at the Hanoi Hilton are singularly instructive. Despite repeated articulations that all she really wanted at the shelter was a place to sleep at night and to keep her things, she was required to attend case management sessions that directly interfered with her education. The shelter staff was adhering to a strict formulaic process, a kind of assembly line approach that equates clients to widgets, without trying to understand or appreciate where Michelle was coming from or what she wanted. Instead of helping her proceed with her education, the staff tried to push her into job readiness and job training, even though she had a good employment history and expressed no need for that type of training. As she indicates in her story, "There is something about the nature of a system of the people saying they are there to help you and yet they are the very ones causing you agony. How can they help you when they never ask what it is that you need?"

The need for a trauma-informed, client-centered approach is even more critical for populations with special needs. Persons with a disability, seniors, and veterans, especially those with PTSD, who are experiencing homelessness, need particular attention. The entire homelessness service system must realize that a single prescribed approach to homelessness is only one among a wide variety of options. The staff must learn to ask questions, to listen, to be flexible in how they work with their clients. Furthermore, when a client indicates a need for more safety, as Michelle did, eviction is not the correct response. Patience and flexibility are absolute requirements; reacting in anger is not productive or ethical.

Racial Bias

Throughout her story, there are explicit indicators of racial bias. When Michelle first arrived in the Denver area, she tried to find a job, and several potential employers discriminated against her because she was black. Later on, when she experienced extreme frustration with her case managers about their insistence that she attend their training sessions rather than go to her required classes at UCD, she asked her school counselor, a white male, to go with her to meet the case managers. "WTF, the power of a white male never ends, even if it is used for a black homeless female. I pimped him out to get what I needed. You see, they never heard me when I said the very same thing; I was invisible and voiceless because if you are roofless, you have no choice, no sense, and no value. Like I said, I am black; how can I be invisible?"

Racial bias pervades homelessness. As we indicated in Chapter 1, African Americans constitute over 40 percent of the total population of those experiencing homelessness, more than three times their percentage of the total US population. Hispanics, Pacific Islanders, native Hawaiians, Native Americans, and Alaskan Natives are also overrepresented. These differences are the result of racial and cultural discrimination in all sectors of our society (Olivet & Dones, 2018).

Ownership of a home is one fundamental way to build family assets. Even here, there are significant differences between African Americans and whites; for whites homeownership is approximately 30 percent higher than African American homeownership, contributing to the fact that the median family wealth of a white family is nearly ten times that of the median African American family (Jones, Schmitt, & Wilson, 2018).

Jones, Schmitt, and Wilson (2018) also found that while progress has been made in the African American community over the past fifty years, there is still a substantial lag in progress toward closing the education and wage gaps as a result of several factors. To date, African

Americans only make 82.5 cents per dollar of their white counterparts. Their rate of poverty is also 2.5 times higher than whites'. In 2013, the salaries of two in five Hispanic workers and more than one of every three black workers were at poverty level. However, less than one in four white workers earned this same poverty level of income in 2013, and this percent continues to decline, widening income inequality in this nation (Hardin, 2016).

This widening income gap is due in part to the disproportionate level of educational attainment and the subsequent decreased earning potential of African Americans. While the high school graduation rate between African Americans and whites has narrowed, in examining college completion rates, the gap has remained largely unchanged for over fifty years. African Americans earn college degrees at about half the rate of white students in this country.

However, as the 2018 study conducted by SPARC (Supporting Partnerships for Anti-Racist Communities) pointed out, the overrepresentation of black Americans in the homeless population cannot be solely explained by poverty (Olivet et al., 2018). They are 13 percent of the population, 26 percent of those living in poverty, yet they comprise over 40 percent of people experiencing homelessness. If poverty were solely responsible, there would be closer alignment between poverty and homelessness rates, yet there remains a statistically significant overrepresentation.

All of this suggests that, despite the legal desegregation of public education almost sixty-five years ago and the creation of the Great Society and federal rulings about housing segregation some ten years later, there is still rampant racial bias, racial profiling, and discrimination throughout the country. We must find more effective ways to address this issue if we are going to become a truly inclusive society in which everyone has equal opportunity to succeed.

Other Factors

SPARC also found other factors such as family disintegration, behavioral health, and network impoverishment to be catalysts into and barriers from exiting homelessness (Olivet et al., 2018). Systems such as child welfare and juvenile justice were named, along with the criminal justice system, as contributing to family disintegration. Early pregnancy, domestic violence, and intimate partner violence also contributed significantly to disruption of family stability. Family networks often had insufficient resources to provide much help, leading to what SPARC called "network impoverishment" (Olivet et al., 2018, p. 12).

Caring Friends and Networks of Support

Finally, Michelle's story reinforces the centrality of caring friends and a strong support community. Cameron and Izzy were crucial for her ability to weather the storm of homelessness, and the Vet Center and the Boots to Suits group also played vital roles in her progress in ultimately finding housing and steady employment.

We cannot emphasize this enough. The human touch, social capital, natural supports—call it what you will—are a common thread through all our stories, and they should not be underestimated. In short, people experiencing homelessness need many resources, like housing, health and behavioral health care services, assistance with job training and job placement, trauma-informed care, and so on, but they also need human resources, social capital, caring individuals, networks of support, and community. These resources are essential for people to avoid entering homelessness or to escape homelessness if they are already there.

Note

An earlier version of Michelle's story first appeared in *Ending Homelessness: Why We Haven't, How We Can* (Burnes & DiLeo, 2016).

9

Someone Who Listens: James's Journey

Here is a perfect example of how a terminal illness, an adult's willingness to care for a very sick parent, and a very antagonistic familial relationship can lead to homelessness. Once again, our storyteller, James, does not fit the homelessness stereotype, but he ends up without a home nevertheless. His experiences in his legal battle with his sister indicate the vagaries of our legal system for those facing evictions and homelessness and the need for various parts of the system to listen to the client. His initial unsuccessful efforts to find an apartment, even with housing assistance, highlight current faults in our housing system.

James's Story

My Mother, Family Discord, and the Court

As an introduction to my odyssey into homelessness, I'd like to qualify it as being just that: a story of my experience. Here is some background information that may help you to better understand how I (or you, or someone you may know) could fall into an unfortunate predicament such as homelessness. I had first left employment to care for my terminally ill father and then for my terminally ill mother, and throughout the experience of caring for her during her last days, my sister continually tried to undermine my efforts and ability to do so.

Her actions to undermine my efforts to care for our mother started with calling Adult Protective Services (APS) and making false charges against me, bringing into question my capabilities and motives for caring for our mother. The case was closed after two compulsory visits. My sister then, acting as my mother's power of attorney, filed a lawsuit on behalf of my mother charging me basically with the same complaints she made to APS, plus, for the sake of litigation, the formal charge of using my mother's illness for personal gain. In response, I decided to represent myself in the legal proceedings.

There were three provisions in the final resolution, drawn up mostly by my sister's lawyers with minor input from the court-appointed surrogates, that I felt I could not live with or accept. One, that I leave the premises within two months of our mother either dying or moving from her home; two, that my stipend (for caring for our mother) be cut off immediately following our mother no longer living in her home; and lastly, that my sister be given final medical authority over our mother.

I felt it was reasonable for me to request adequate time to recuperate following my mother's death, and to have the stipend continued for another month or two so that I would have money to live on and be able to pay for another place to live while I transitioned. The final medical authority to me was absurd. My sister was still in denial that there was anything seriously wrong with our mother despite the court declaring her incompetent to handle her own affairs any longer due to dementia. We wouldn't have even been in court if our mother could still take care of herself.

So, I went forward with my request for a hearing before the judge. We marched back into the courtroom, took our places, and my sister's lawyer then spoke first and announced to the judge that if I refused to sign the resolution, they would make a motion to have our mother taken out of our care and placed in a nursing home or another institution for the ill and aging. I was shocked and wasn't even going to take it seriously until the judge asked my sister's lawyer if they had specific places to recommend. When they responded that they did, I spoke up and said that I would accept the resolution as is.

The whole purpose for me taking care of our mother at home was so that she could avoid the experience of going into a nursing home and enduring impersonal care. It was her greatest fear and something I had promised her I would never let happen. I couldn't compromise on that, so I reluctantly agreed to sign the resolution.

A Trip into a Rabbit Hole or the Safety Net: Pick Your Poison

When I got home from my mother's funeral, I called my former case manager at social services. When I explained what was happening, she advised me to come in right away and renew my general assistance application. Once I was approved for general assistance again, I could then go to emergency housing and ask for rental aid.

I reopened my case and then walked over to the offices of emergency housing (all of the various social service agencies are clustered in one large nondescript building complex barely noticeable from the street or average passerby). Like most people, I had no idea they were there until I had to. There I learned that one is not homeless just because they don't have a place to live or, as in my case, they know they will soon no longer have a place to live. A person is *legally* homeless and entitled to consideration for housing assistance *only if they can prove that they can no longer live in their present residence through no fault of their own.* Even though I knew that I would soon be without a place to live, I could not receive housing assistance without having something specific in writing stating that I could no longer live there after a certain date.

I filed another legal motion contesting the provision of the resolution that stated I had to be out of the house in less than a month. I protested on the grounds that the house had not been sold yet and I wasn't ready to leave. The judge said that I had to live by what I signed and that was that. He ordered me evicted from the house by a specific date—a month and a half later than what my sister wanted so that I wouldn't have to leave "in the middle of the holidays." I would get a formal eviction notice delivered to me in the mail.

I knew that I would not be ready to leave by then—financially or emotionally. General assistance was providing me with $140 a month, and I had but a meager amount of money left from the holiday sales of my e-book, *An American Yoga: The Kripalu Story* (Abro, 2011). Combined together they were not nearly enough to pay rent on an apartment in the area, let alone the required deposit and additional month's rent. I couldn't get back to work editing books just like that. I needed time to make new contacts. Plus, I just wasn't feeling right. I had trouble concentrating for any length of time, and in general, I felt uneasy and unsure of myself. I certainly did not feel like the same person who just a few months ago was taking on whatever Alzheimer's threw at him confidently while working on a book in between tasks.

The vague but palpable anxiety I was feeling had crept up on me gradually over the last few months so in some ways I had come to accept it as my "new normal." Therefore, it wasn't easy to do, but one morning I drove myself to the emergency room of the nearest hospital. They took me into a screening room off the lobby to check my blood pressure. After they checked my blood pressure again, they admitted me to a triage unit where they monitored me for a possible stroke. They began asking questions about what had been going on in my life recently. They listened and then admitted me to a private room in the hospital. There, a physician met with me and told me that he thought I could be experiencing an anxiety disorder caused by the trauma of losing my mother. They gave me a sedative and let me rest until my blood pressure was back to normal. Then they released me with the advice to contact the local mental health clinic for further analysis, counseling, and treatment. How I was feeling was starting to scare me. So, I went home, called the clinic, and was put on a waiting list—it usually took about three months to see a counselor and psychiatrist, "unless you were thinking of harming yourself or someone else." I wasn't.

There was nothing more I knew I could do about that now. My eviction date was getting closer, and I would have to put aside for now how I was feeling and focus, as best I could, on getting it together in order to secure some place to live after I had to move out of the house. I returned to Emergency Housing Services with the eviction notice and was told by them that they'd put me up in a motel for up to three months, during which time I was supposed to find more suitable permanent housing, which the state would then subsidize for up to a year (under a certain dollar amount). They gave me forms to give to landlords to fill out stating that they were willing to accept public-financed renters.

I visited several apartment complexes in my immediate vicinity. Without exception, none of them would agree to sign the forms. Some didn't want to because they claimed that they would then be required to accept anyone the state sent them. Others complained that the state took too long to pay. Others simply didn't want to be bothered. There was no enforcement or incentive for landlords to accept the forms.

You are not homeless until you finally leave your home for good. I waited for a friend to come by; the friend lived in Vermont and was visiting friends and family in New Jersey. I told him how I was feeling and that I didn't want to move out of my home for good by myself. He understood. I had also told him about a quaint little church I had discovered, and he said that he'd like to go and check it out. It was a Sunday, so we did. I was in no hurry to get to the motel and my friend was up for anything "spiritual."

I don't recall what the church service was about, though I do remember introducing my friend to the pastor and that they seemed to "connect." I was glad to be among friendly faces, even if I didn't yet know any of them very well. The church would be at least one place, once a week, that I could look forward to going to. I'm sure I didn't tell anyone in the congregation that I'd been evicted from my home by my sister, and that I'd be staying in a motel nearly an hour away indefinitely. I don't think I even really believed it yet. The whole event was more than just a bit unreal. A woman there mentioned a possible apartment.

I'd driven out to the motel earlier in the week to pick up my key and see what it looked like. But looking at it and moving into it were two different things. It had one large double bed that took up most of the room, a chair, a table with a TV on it, a small refrigerator, and a microwave. There was a four-by-four bathroom with a shower, and an open closet space with hangers. A single small chest of drawers. The room reeked of stale cigarette smoke, and despair. Set atop the chest of drawers was a piece of paper with the "house rules" typed on it. They included "no overnight guests." As if?

I felt the air go out of me and my mood sunk even lower; the anxiety became nearly paralyzing. One of the most difficult and abrupt adjustments I was being forced to make was going from a life that was fully engaged, challenging, and fulfilling—supervising the in-home care of my mother throughout the course of her illness—to one where I had to more or less sit back, wait for things to happen and change, and have faith that they would.

The faith that I had at this time that things would change for the better was not strong, to say the least. For one thing, I was still going through the early stages of grief, including feeling anger and shock that someone I loved and cared for was just taken away. Plus, I was reeling from stress and emotional trauma, which makes one's outlook on life seem anything but confident and hopeful.

A Bright Spot on the Horizon

When I spoke to the woman from church again, and I was calling her every day, she informed me that as far as she knew the apartment was still available. So, I drove out to see it and meet with the landlord so that I could assure him in person that I was doing everything I could to expedite the matter through social services. After seeing the apartment, I wanted it that much more and was that much more afraid of "losing it." The apartment was in an older building—built circa 1940—and well maintained. Plus, it was located in the downtown area of the same town I was living in while taking care of my mother. I missed getting in at the beginning of the month and tried to continue my routine from the motel as best I could. Medical universities in urban environments don't close easily or for long during storms like the one we were in, and cab companies don't make money if they are not driving, so I was able to keep my dental appointments. The student atmosphere there was lively, optimistic, and uplifting—a nice change of scene for at least a few hours or so.

I also met with my caseworker in social services, who assured me that I would be able to move into the apartment in the middle of the month. It is not a given, even if you have all the necessary paperwork, to receive housing assistance from the state. I knew this going into the experience, so I tried to approach the task in the same manner I would a job interview. I went to the meetings with my caseworker well-groomed and well-dressed, and, more importantly, I knew exactly what I wanted to get from social services and what I needed to have in order to obtain it. I went to the meetings prepared. I also approached my caseworker differently than I saw others doing. Instead of bringing a laundry list of problems I needed solving, I narrowed it down to what I most needed immediately and asked for only that. In my case, housing assistance.

As part of my move into my new apartment, I got a couple of people with pickup trucks who were willing to help me move my bed from my uncle's garage to the apartment, but they were still busy using their trucks to help sweep away the remains of the snowstorm from large commercial properties. According to the news (though who believed their hyperventilating weather reports any longer?), it had been the worst storm in a decade. So, there was money to be made by anyone with a truck and plow. I understood that. What an auspicious day for a new start.

The Future

Since stabilizing my housing and financial situations, I have been on a mission to answer the question raised by the title of Donald Burnes's book, *Ending Homelessness: Why We Haven't, How We Can* (2016). I now volunteer at the same community outreach to the poor and homeless that helped me when I needed support. So, this is not an academic issue for me. In addition to my hands-on experience of working with the homeless, I have also studied the economic, political, and social aspects of acute poverty in America. This has resulted in the publication of more than a dozen of my articles in *The Nation* magazine and by progressive political organizations.

What I want to do in the near future is combine my experience and knowledge of poverty and homelessness in order to collaborate on creating a working model that will allow communities, on their own, to significantly reduce poverty where they live and work. After fifty-plus years of trying top-down government solutions to this condition, I strongly believe it's time to return the management to the communities where poverty and homelessness exist, and I have practical ideas on how we can make this work.

Implications

Adequate Legal Representation

This is a story about the unfortunate juxtaposition of a son's commitment to provide ongoing care for terminally ill parents on the one hand and the bitter struggle with a sister over control of their mother's final days on the other. James left a self-sufficient life of writing and editing to care first for an ailing father and then for his terminally ill mother, assuming that he would be rewarded for his assistance by some portion of the inheritance and by use of his parents' home on the New Jersey shore. After a series of legal battles with his sister in which he received bad legal advice and was finally ordered to leave the house within a short period of time with little or no compensation for his efforts to help his parents, he was forced to rely on local services to acquire housing and some modest financial support.

The death of a parent and the disposition of the resulting family resources are often the recipe for bitter internecine family disputes. That certainly was the case here, as basic underlying disagreements between siblings advanced to the fore. In this particular instance, the sister had greater familiarity with the law and with the local conditions, thereby putting James at a significant disadvantage. In addition, James engaged the legal system by himself, further circumscribing his ability to present his case.

One of the clear implications of James's story is the need for adequate legal representation. He did approach Legal Aid to get advice about his situation, and, in retrospect, he was not given good advice. However, Legal Aid could not accompany him into the courtroom, and, as James later said, "The problem is that they can't represent you in court, which is when you need them the most." James admits that, in a conversation with a lawyer friend of his, he was informed that the sister's threats to remove his mother to a nursing home, an outcome that James had promised his mother he would not allow to happen, was in all likelihood a bluff. Appropriate legal representation in court would have realized this and would have responded differently from the way James did, thus changing the potential outcome of the dispute that ultimately resulted in his becoming homeless.

The need for adequate legal representation is an altogether familiar story in the homelessness arena. Therefore, we must figure out a way for tenants, and in James's case the current inhabitant of a building, to have access to adequate legal representation. This is particularly important when the individual in question is suffering from a debilitating illness, as James was at the time. James describes himself as approaching a nervous breakdown, certainly suffering from a severe case of PTSD, and he was in no condition to represent himself in a court of law. It is very likely that the outcome of the legal battle would have been very different if he had had an attorney.

Listening to the Voice of Lived Experience

A theme that runs through James's story is the strong need for service agencies and case managers to listen to and hear their clients' articulations of their stories, their needs, and their suggestions for how to move forward. As James said in additional comments, "The first rule of law is that there are no rules. People working with the homeless often make the mistake of thinking that 'the homeless' are all alike, suffering from the same maladies that are causing their setbacks."

In addition, case managers sometimes have the tendency to consider themselves the experts and to make recommendations without really listening to and understanding where the client is coming from. In their chapter in *Ending Homelessness* entitled "Controversies in the Provision of Services," Wasserman and Clair (2016) described this phenomenon as the medical model approach to homeless services, as in the doctor knows best how to cure a patient's medical issue. Although James finally found an apartment through the efforts of a local agency, it took a long time and there were many complications, in part because the case manager did not take the time to fully understand James's situation.

As was the case with Michelle in the previous chapter, some case managers approach their work as the need to check off successes on their evaluation sheet. For them, going through the motions and completing the appropriate process are both more important than truly understanding their clients' needs and wants and working toward their clients' hopes and expectations. Therefore, it is imperative that case managers and agency leaders focus on their clients rather than on some scorecard, always listening and hearing where their clients are coming from.

James relates, "An author friend of mine, Tonier Cain, describes in her book *Healing Neen* (2014) how she struggled for decades with homelessness, drug addiction, incarcerations, and didn't start the healing process until a 'trauma therapist' sat down across from her, looked her in the eye, and questioned her very directly." According to James,

> This can't be emphasized enough. It will not only allow the person in distress to unburden themselves, it will allow you to earn their trust and respect. But as individuals working with the homeless, we can discard the generalities and hone in on who each person is, what got them into this situation, and what *they* think they need to overcome it. This last step is vitally important. I recall,

when I first became homeless, how baffling it was to have people's perceptions of me change in an instant, from being admired for hanging in there and taking care of my terminally ill mother at home through all the stages of Alzheimer's, to someone people simply brushed off as either having something wrong with them or doing something wrong.

What better statement of the need for case managers and other service agency staff to take the time to really get to know their clients! In fact, this admonition goes for all of us. It is imperative for each of us to really get to know individuals who have experienced homelessness so that we can have a better understanding and appreciation for what their lives are like and for what they need, what they want, and what their hopes and dreams are. This can be truly transformative.

In summary, as James said,

Find the people in your community who have dealt with homelessness and overcome it. They are your real experts. Treat the homeless you encounter with care and respect, and, most importantly, let them know that you are on their side. Your motto should be that no matter what mistakes a person made to get into the situation of facing homelessness, no one in America deserves to live the nightmare of homelessness.

The Importance of Community

One of the important lessons from James's story is the role that his church community provided: a place of peace, friendship, and community throughout his ordeal. Although it was a local service agency that helped him find and pay for a motel room, it was a friend of his from his church community that actually identified the apartment he ultimately moved into. Friends from his church helped him move, and they were critical for James as he recovered from the stress of his situation. Subsequently, James formed a real bond with the pastor; he helps out in their community outreach efforts; and he has given more than one presentation to the congregation about his experiences and their role in assisting him.

While we are not suggesting that everyone who is experiencing homelessness should gravitate toward a spiritual community, congregations can often provide a real sense of community and belonging. What we are suggesting is that creating natural support groups and supportive communities is a central element in providing a path out of homelessness.

10

Improved Health Care: Caroline's Journey

The final story in the collection is written by a woman who became unhoused because of a medical condition. At one point in her career, she was a six-figure senior staff person at a major company with a nice home, good medical insurance, and a very rosy future. Felled by undiagnosed Lyme disease and a strong reaction to mold, she lost her health, 20 percent of her cognitive ability, her job, her savings, and her home.

Unlike the other contributors in our collection, Caroline remains without a home, although a number of people are working to find her a place to live. We include her story for two reasons. First, her story represents an important segment of the population of those experiencing homelessness, that is, a person who is forced into homelessness by an undiagnosed chronic disease and for whom the health-care system has not provided the support she needs. In addition, despite her illness negatively affecting her life for over two years, Caroline has managed to maintain a positive outlook, thanks to a strong support network and some caring individuals, all of whom are among those trying to find her housing.

Caroline's Story

Background

I was as surprised as anyone to find myself in this situation. I willingly believed hard work would carry me through life's pitfalls and pave the way for an essentially comfortable life. I was raised to believe that the world rewards diligence; so, all I had to do was show up, make good choices, and throw my strength into it.

I'd always wondered about the folks I saw on street corners holding a cardboard sign or curled up in a sleeping bag over a steam grate. What happened that led them to this? I never really thought of it as laziness; their existence seemed much more difficult than mine, but I couldn't imagine the spiral that landed them in that spot. I feel like I understand this a little better now. As long as we perpetuate the myth that people without homes have failed in some irreparable way that justifies us turning our backs on them, we kick the issue downfield where we run the risk of running into it again, and maybe end up without homes ourselves.

My Story

In 2015, I landed the big promotion I'd been working toward, reporting as a data analyst to the executive vice president of compliance. I worked with executive and senior-level management translating their initiatives into technical requirements for IT, and procedural requirements for operations. I loved my job! I adored my manager; I had fun projects; led happy, inclusive project groups; and collaborated with every unit, at every level of the company. I finally earned enough to live comfortably, pay down debt, and save for retirement.

A few months into my new job the confusion came. I couldn't seem to grasp where I was or what I was doing. Talking through it with my doctor, it occurred to me that all I'd done for the last year was work and sleep. Months ticked by while we ran all the usual tests and waited for results that didn't show anything remarkable. One morning on the way to work I couldn't understand the traffic signals and caused an accident. I was so confused all the time. I blanked out in the middle of conversations, unable to recover, and then developed periods of paralysis where I was conscious but unable to move or speak. Like a sinkhole, my cognition and mobility quietly slipped out from under me until everything fell apart.

My doctor suggested Lyme disease, and I literally scoffed. How could I possibly have Lyme?! Apparently that weird bug bite I got while hiking in Colorado was a tick bite. Going undiagnosed and untreated for eighteen months, the infection had spread to my brain and was beyond the reach of standard antibiotics. The inflammation was out of control, and while only in my mid-forties, I was experiencing signs of early dementia. My management team at work encouraged me to follow my doctor's advice, take a leave of absence, and focus on my health. I had a great benefits package, including an employer-sponsored disability program that offered income replacement to cover my living expenses and the staggering out-of-pocket medical expenses. The specialized medication and equipment for my treatment protocol wasn't covered by insurance, but I felt like I had it under control. The disability coverage and savings would get me through the four months of treatment and help me get back to work.

Six weeks into my treatment protocol I was much worse. I started to wonder if we were missing something. It's typical to feel worse before you feel better, but even my doctor was concerned. I felt like I'd been electrocuted. Every nerve in my body felt exposed, crispy, and raw. I had excruciating ice-pick headaches, vertigo, and a speech impediment. I had extreme light and noise intolerance, unable to stand the flash of changing images on TV, unable to even listen to music. And I could only whisper, because the vibration of my own voice was too much for my brain. I spent my days curled up under a sheet on the floor of my closet wearing ear plugs and a face mask, waiting for the sun to go down. My cognition was so dim, and I was in so much pain, it honestly felt like a nightmare.

After more tests, we discovered that I was also reacting to the mold and other toxins found in water-damaged buildings. Since Lyme and mold illness are both environmentally acquired biotoxin illnesses, it is quite common for them to present together. Researchers have found that Lyme causes immune dysfunction. The toxins from water-damaged buildings enter the body, cannot be eliminated by the immune system, and trigger inflammation that is multisystemic, attacking every system in the body. With fresh perspective, I looked around at my pretty little condo and realized, to my horror, the walls were full of mold—and my entire central nervous system was on fire.

Since the diagnosis, I have learned that the system most often affected is the central nervous system. Significant brain swelling is common and manifests visibly as air hunger, fatigue, cognitive decline, pain, vertigo, and neuropsychiatric issues. My brain volume scan revealed a critical level of brain swelling, and my neurocognitive evaluation revealed a thirty-point IQ loss.

While my doctors and I scrambled to determine next steps, my employer's disability company denied my claim, simply stating there was no evidence that I was sick or unable to work. Despite the test results and statements from doctors, they rejected it all. Just like that.

Living alone, I drifted in and out of consciousness, too sick to find my way out of this. There was no way I could return to work, and I'd already spent the majority of my savings on the initial treatment that failed. Without an income, the next promising treatment protocol was no longer affordable. I was stranded. Over the next ten months, I wiped out the remainder of my savings and my retirement. I sold all of my furniture to keep the roof over my head—then lost that roof. I got some help from family and friends but not enough to continue the treatment I'd have to pay for out of pocket or to maintain a household. I lost the job I loved and went from a six-figure income to homeless in twelve months.

I quickly discovered that documented physical disability does not necessarily guarantee the receipt of disability income. Yet without it, I'm cut off from the core elements of health: healthy food, safe and clean housing, and meaningful health care. I'd given my life to the American Dream, and in this moment when I really needed to lean on it, it was just that—a dream. There is no safety net, even if you've done all the right things. And yet, failing to do "all the right things" is the first reason given when help is withheld.

When I lost my condo, I was making arrangements to move into my car. At the very last minute I found a HUD-subsidized living facility for the disabled that offered housing on a sliding scale based on income. After an arduous application and board review process they allowed me to see a unit—a 275-square-foot studio in a rundown seventy-year-old building. I realized within a few days that I was reacting to something in the unit. I tried to make the most of it, but my vertigo, fatigue, and migraines were worse than ever. I found black mold on the back wall under my kitchen sink. When I reported it to the management, they refused to fix it, insisting it was "inert" and had no impact on my health. My doctor wrote a letter stating I needed to vacate on medical grounds—and I did.

My best friend's mother offered me a temporary spot in her home until I could figure out something else. As lovely and comfortable as it was, there was water damage there and my health continued to decline. My doctor, at the end of her rope, literally suggested I move into a tent. The outdoor environment was less detrimental for me than living indoors, and I had no income for rent. I was desperate for safe housing.

When all of this occurred, I didn't realize a disability insurance company could just deny a claim backed by reasonable medical evidence. Unbelievably, plans provided by employers are governed by the Federal Employee Retirement Income Security Act of 1974 (ERISA) that actually protects the interests of employers and insurance companies—not employees. The insurance company can, and did, look for reasons to deny my claim, not approve it. The burden of proof was on me, and nothing would be enough. In my starry-eyed version of the American Dream, I never considered an insurance company would refuse to honor their fiduciary duty—and be empowered by a federal law to do so.

These employer-sponsored plans tend to favor definitive illness or injury that can wrap up in about twelve weeks—with treatments that follow a well-worn groove in our medical system and typically result in a return to work. Little did I know that chronic illness falls through the cracks. The ill-defined, unpredictable symptoms, tests, and treatment plans give the insurance companies a way out. However, the meaningful treatment protocols required when Lyme reaches a chronic state can only be obtained by paying out of pocket. This puts them out of reach of many, implying one gets all the health care they can afford.

When you look at the social determinants of health, I had everything going for me. I was a well-educated, high-wage earner. I had a home, access to health care, and loving, supportive relationships. I'd done all the right things. I'd signed up for all of my employer's benefits, which consisted of a well-rounded combination of retirement and health savings, along with health, life, and disability insurance. I was living beneath my means and putting money away above and beyond my retirement accounts. I don't drink, smoke, or do drugs of any kind. I got regular checkups, ate well, took my vitamins, and lived an active lifestyle. When I became ill, I sought the advice of specialists and took their medical advice. The week before I went out on leave, I had a great performance review, and the monetary reward to go with it. What had I missed? What else was I supposed to have done?

There is no meaningful safety net, because there is a cultural assumption that poverty, illness, and homelessness are the result of personal failing. There is so much emphasis on developing individuals so they can acquire the social determinants of health. Yet there is no discussion about how to support those who had everything until a health crisis that couldn't be mitigated by a healthy lifestyle, a good job, and health insurance took them down.

My Community's Response

I wasn't prepared for how lonely this process would be. I'm an independent, resourceful soul, but I connect deeply with people. Everyone matters to me. I work hard to balance my roles as a loving, committed family member, friend, and neighbor—while standing on my own two feet. So, I'm comfortable in my aloneness, but this new loneliness is different. The social isolation of chronic illness is suffocating. I'm an action-oriented individual, and I'm trapped in a body I no longer recognize, with no obvious way out. I've lost everything that made me who I am. I built my life with plucky determination, intellect, ingenuity, and some solid interpersonal skills. But who am I now? What am I, if I can't even lift a gallon of water by myself? Or do basic math? Or figure out which agency or volunteer organization can help me?

The people in my life didn't understand any of this. Shortly after my initial treatment failed, my friends and family began doubting my illness. They too had a hard time believing an insurance company would arbitrarily deny a claim. So, when I further reported that doctors who take insurance will not diagnose or treat mold and Lyme, my fate was sealed. To my horror, they concluded there must not be enough medical evidence to prove I'm sick. They threw out everything they knew about me and my life up to that point and decided I must be faking it or experiencing some kind of mental break.

Every time I hit a roadblock and asked for help, the people in my world acted like it wasn't real. They suggested I just hadn't reached the right person, at the right agency, or hadn't asked the right question. When their quick-fix suggestions failed to solve my mounting problems, they disappeared. They were desperate to believe there were "services" out there for me. They were desperate to believe that every problem has a solution—provided by the government, not them. So, if I couldn't find the solution, then I must be the problem. With total disregard for me and what my condition requires, they wanted me to go to a shelter because that's what made them comfortable. They needed me to be in a box they understood, so they could feel better about what was happening to me. None of them was willing to admit my problems could only be solved at the grassroots level. When I held out for a solution that would actually support me, they walked away.

My community's lack of understanding about invisible illness and how it's treated by the insurance and medical communities would turn out to be one of the greatest contributing factors to my homelessness. In some ways, this whole process would have been easier if I had cancer, multiple sclerosis, or lupus—not because they are less terrible or somehow desirable, but because more people have a frame of reference for them. Being unrelatable cost me the social support I'd need to survive.

People are always asking, "Where is your family?" There is an expectation that my family should, and would, be compelled to step in and help if I were truly sick. When I say that my family just isn't interested in helping me, there's an assumption that I've done something to warrant their loss of favor, but I just got sick. No one in my family is interested in meeting with my doctors or my attorney, who would willingly walk them through the severity of my situation. None of them asked if I needed a ride to my weekly infusions. And my father said that he was unwilling to help me with living or treatment expenses because he considers me a lost cause, not worth wasting his money. He did eventually help me somewhat, but it only drew more animosity from my siblings.

Crumbs from the Benefit Table

I've been out of work for twenty-six months. The insurance company just now settled out of court for the first eleven weeks of my disability, and they paid 30 cents on the dollar. Out of that, I paid taxes and attorney's fees and will owe more taxes because the payment was coded as a settlement rather than insurance disbursement as it would have been had they just paid me when I filed. We're now working with the insurance company on the last twenty-four months I've been out of work. There is no way to know how long they'll drag out the appeal and arbitration process. The monthly benefit amount I was due to receive would have been enough to cover my living expenses and out-of-pocket medical expenses. Had they just paid out my policy when I filed the claim, I'd probably be back at work by now. And I definitely wouldn't be homeless.

I filed for Social Security Disability but was denied on an administrative technicality in my initial filing. Apparently, that's standard and there's no "emergency disability" payment while I wait eighteen months for an appeal hearing. As I write this, I'm nine months into the eighteen-month wait. And there's no guarantee I'll actually get it. I know people who have been fighting to get their benefit for more than five years. I reached out to the Department of Health and Human Services for help. As a single female without children I qualify for $192 of food stamps (SNAP) per month and $185 in Aid to the Needy and Disabled (AND), which is a cash program. That's all. I can visit the county food bank twice in six weeks. If I make (or receive as a gift) more than $900 per month, I lose food stamps. If I make or receive any money as a gift, it is deducted from the $185 of AND. Those with spouses and children receive greater cash assistance and are allowed at the food bank more often. But I, as a single female, do not qualify.

What is the fate of our American workforce when hundreds of thousands of healthy, capable people in the prime of their lives are felled by an illness modern medicine just doesn't have a plan for, and insurance companies don't acknowledge?

What Saved Me?

I'm still unstably housed, but I'm not sure I'd still be alive if I was trying to do this without my faith. I found myself asking very serious questions. Who am I when I can't show up as the person I used to be? Do I have anything to offer if I'm not a working professional? Do I matter, if I don't have anything to give? Am I allowed to exist, if I have nothing to offer? What's the point of my existence?

Right after I was diagnosed with Lyme, I met with a Lyme advocate who told me, "If I didn't have my wife and kids, I would've killed myself. This is just too hard to go through alone, and for no reason." I was shocked. It seemed so extreme at the moment, but I understand it now. The combined effect of brain swelling, so severe it alters your personality, and profound social isolation, is the perfect recipe for suicide. Suicide is the leading cause of death for Lyme disease and mold illness.

I got really honest with myself and made my way down the list of hard questions. I knew in my heart I'd done nothing to bring this on myself and genuinely sought a better-than-ever recovery. When I took the questions to God, I heard quite clearly that I am perfect, exactly as I am—even sick, poor, and homeless. I don't need to be or do anything else. The end. I accepted the realities of my limits and focused on what I could do, rather than mourn what I couldn't.

I turned to my local Lyme/mold support group for information, ideas, and moral support. I'd never been involved in a support group, preferring to figure things out on my own. I really resisted leaning in there, but when I finally did, I was amazed by what I found. I was surrounded by really smart, kind, motivated professionals who were already a few steps ahead. They understood the complexity of the illness, they understood the symptoms, they understood the isolation, they understood the complete breakdown of life as we knew it . . . and they were all looking for a way through it too. They had so much information! And they held space for me to be whatever I needed to be, whenever I needed it. I didn't have to justify anything to them. They know I'm doing the best I can, and they cheer me on. They didn't judge me on my bad days as though I'll never be well again, nor did they judge me on my good days, as though I'm done healing and ready to get on with life. They understand it's a rollercoaster and all you can do is your best.

My new community isn't afraid to sit down with me and hear about my day, good or bad. And I'm not afraid to hear about theirs. They know they can say anything to me and I'll be in it with them. We know it's a mixed bag of really difficult things, and astonishingly wonderful things—and they all matter.

At the absolute worst time in my life, I am the happiest I've ever been. I don't know if it's because I feel like I don't have anything else to lose, or I just don't have the energy to wring my hands, but I cannot tell you how relieved I am to discover that when things are at their worst, my default response is joy and loving kindness. I love deeply and fully just because it feels good. I speak my truth and set healthy boundaries, which lets everyone around me off the hook for "figuring out" what I'm available for. I reach out with loving support to lift others up when they don't know which way to go, and I let myself be vulnerable with them.

Don's faith in me was my second big turning point. I'd seen him on the news, picked up the phone, and called him. "Mr. Burnes, are the toxins present in water-damaged buildings on your radar when considering housing options for those without homes?" He said, "They are now!" As we spoke, he immediately believed me and understood the implications. He offered insight, ideas, and real contacts to help me find shelter and further my efforts as an advocate. He did not presume to build a solution for me; he shared his strength to help me build the solution I needed. For the first time in years, the solution architect in me felt like I had some traction. I didn't have the energy to pursue it as I would normally, but I had little chunks I could work on when I had the strength. It gave me something to act on, which made all the other waiting on doctors and insurance companies more bearable.

Then he asked me to participate in this book. I noticed how much of my grieving stemmed from being blamed and demeaned for something I had no control over, until someone from the real world held space for me. My suffering felt invisible and meaningless to all the healthy people in my community. He understood my frustration around their presumption that my situation is the result of personal failing, and fear that they might miss the big point: this could happen to them. So, when Don offered me an opportunity to tell my story, and potentially help others learn from my experience, it was the greatest gift he could've given me.

My work with Don also opened doors with other groups who asked me to share my story in a series of public speaking engagements. And most recently we've begun discussing how to manifest my crazy little dream of a tiny-home village of safe, clean houses for those of us with Lyme and environmentally acquired illness. It's amazing to look back over the last two years and see how much good has come from such a painful experience.

I'm a human spirit junkie. I am drawn to moments of crisis, not because I enjoy the adrenaline rush or seeing others suffer. I am drawn by the strength I know I'll see when I, or the one across from me, is stripped of everything but their basic humanity and the enduring human spirit takes over. When we turn toward these moments and make space for the wonder of this experience it's utterly intoxicating. We feel bigger, stronger, more connected, more relevant—because even the act of witnessing is performing a powerful role. We receive as much as we give. The adversity we experience ourselves, or witness for others, is an opportunity to deepen our understanding of the world, our relationships, our faith, and our sense of self. And weirdly enough the world starts to feel sweeter and safer, not less. Don't we all want more of that?

I am so relieved when someone is inspired by my story, not because I've pulled myself up, but because I've worked so hard to find beauty and value right where I am. Our culture is starving for the authenticity of emotionally honest moments. Luckily, the solution is as easy as turning toward another in crisis and honoring their sheer will to survive it.

Implications

It Can Happen to Any of Us

Almost more than anything else, Caroline's story is a blunt reminder that the condition of homelessness *really can* happen to almost anyone. A successful midcareer, high-ranking private sector official, Caroline was knocked down by a tick bite that went misdiagnosed for an extended period of time and by additional misdiagnoses of mold susceptibility. The failure of the medical profession to diagnose her illnesses correctly and of the insurance industry to provide appropriate and adequate reimbursement for her medical treatment forced her into living without a home of her own. To make matters worse, her family and her friends decided that she wasn't really sick after all and consequently provided little assistance. What's more, after twenty-six months, because of her precarious financial situation and her specialized housing needs, Caroline is still trying desperately to find some kind of housing accommodation that will prove satisfactory.

As Caroline discovered, she was one, or two, or three paychecks away from housing disaster, like many of the rest of us. Consider what would happen if you, the reader, suffered a major medical catastrophe or if you faced a major natural disaster, like a flood, a hurricane, an earthquake, or a tornado. What would your circumstances be like; would you be able to uncover sufficient resources to maintain your housing and live reasonably comfortably?

As we reported earlier, according to a recent study commissioned by the Board of Governors of the Federal Reserve (2017), almost half of the people interviewed in the study would have to borrow money or utilize a line of credit if they were faced with an unexpected bill of $400 or more, a mere pittance if one considers a car repair or a trip to the hospital or medical clinic. People experiencing homelessness or those in extreme poverty don't have lines of credit, and they cannot borrow money; they are faced with extreme financial dislocation and homelessness. In short, are many of us in fact living on the knife's edge of financial and housing disaster?

The Medical Profession and Medical Insurance

In her implications, Caroline wrote,

> The CDC estimates 300,000 people per year are infected with Lyme disease (US Department of Health and Human Services, 2018). However, doctors and scientists tracking and researching tick-borne illness believe the actual rate of infection is much higher, as much as three times. Given that the current blood test recommended by the CDC isn't sensitive enough to detect all the potential strains of borreliosis, and there is no actual test for chronic fatigue or fibromyalgia, many doctors suspect that these conditions are misdiagnosed borreliosis infections. Thankfully, the US Department of Health and Human Services is finally taking Lyme disease seriously and has put forth the goal of pro-

viding recommendations on a "federal response to tick-borne disease prevention, treatment and research, as well as how to address gaps in those areas" (2018, p. 1). It established the Tick-Borne Disease Working Group comprised of federal and public professionals who represent a broad spectrum of roles and perspectives on working with tick-borne diseases.

Later in her implications, Caroline indicates that the discussion around mold illness, or environmentally acquired illness, is growing. In her 2017 article in *Psychology Today*, Judy Tsafrir linked mold illness to mental health issues, and Dale Bredesen (2016) suggested the mycotoxins created in water-damaged buildings are a potential source of type 3 Alzheimer's—inhalation disease: an unrecognized—and treatable—epidemic. Furthermore, Caroline writes,

> Doctors and researchers familiar with environmentally acquired illness attribute it to a genetic mutation found in 25 percent of the population. The other 75 percent may only notice some basic irritation in a water-damaged building, if anything at all. However, for those of us with mold illness, even trace amounts of indoor mold and other neurotoxins growing in the drywall, carpet, and wood become life altering. Many are suffering, but it's often diagnosed as autism, dementia, arthritis, ADHD, chronic fatigue, fibromyalgia, or mental illness to name a few. The CDC stated in a National Institute for Occupational Safety and Health (NIOSH) report (2012) that 50 percent of the buildings in the United States have a level of water damage that will cause health problems in this vulnerable section of the population.

Caroline's story accentuates the difference between short-term and even terminal illnesses on the one hand and long-term chronic illnesses on the other. Caroline also speaks to the loneliness that accompanies this experience. Her situation, battling a chronic illness, provides an additional layer of complexity as many people doubted her disability. At first, friends organized meals, saying what she needed to hear. In time, after it became apparent her condition could not be solved quickly, this support began to wane. This support began to shift to frustration and blame, ultimately leading to them disengaging. Caroline says it most succinctly: "It's a cruel irony: I'm traumatized by an illness I can't heal or control, those around me won't acknowledge it or offer support, and then they abandoned me when I couldn't keep up." In other words, her network of support, her community, dissolved.

Having spent countless hours with Caroline in the crafting of her chapter, it is easy for us to identify why her network had difficulty connecting her illness to her current housing situation. She is articulate, thoughtful, seemingly capable, and has developed a toolbox of coping skills that many of us can only dream of. She uses SAT words, can explain the complexities of our entire health-care system, and in the course of conversation, speaks to a variety of topics in such detail that one might easily mistake her for a medical doctor. However, after an hour or two, her cognition declines visibly. She begins to lose her ability to retrieve words, fatigue sets in, a headache sometimes emerges, and it is almost as if she begins to wilt. Meetings to discuss her contribution to this book had to occur when she was well-rested so that we had a precious one- to two-hour window of full Caroline brain power. If one only met Caroline during her full-tank moments, it would be easy to see why people doubt her illness. Actually witnessing what she lives with on a day-to-day basis takes spending extended periods of time with her, something many in her network are no longer willing to do. Thankfully, she now has found a support group, a network of people who understand her struggle after their own firsthand experiences down a similar path.

Caroline's story has major significance for all those experiencing homelessness, since the number of them who suffer from some sort of disabling condition is staggering. In 2017, about a quarter of the individuals meeting HUD's definition of homelessness were chronically homeless, or 86,962 people (National Alliance to End Homelessness, 2018a). Chronically homeless, by definition, means these individuals have "experienced homelessness for at least a year—or repeatedly— while struggling with a disabling condition such as a serious mental illness, substance use disorder, or physical disability" (National Alliance to End Homeless, 2018a, para. 1). The vast majority, about 70 percent of them, were living on the street, in a vehicle, or in places like parks or other locations not meant for human habitation.

In her implications, Caroline argues for a single-payer, nonprofit system to allow more room for individualized protocols and lowering the cost to consumers. She contends that we cannot "perpetuate a medical system that is clearly stacked against meaningful health care" and states it is not only "inhumane" but also "bad business," advocating for a shift away from this being viewed as charity and instead viewing this as a basic standard of care.

There must be major reforms in how both the medical profession and insurance carriers respond to various disabilities, especially chronic illnesses, so that every person experiencing homelessness who has a disabling condition receives better medical care and more reimbursements from insurance, when individuals are able to carry it. As part of these reforms, one immediate implication for the medical profession is to advance its understanding of environmentally acquired illnesses like Lyme disease and mold toxicity as soon as possible. The number of people affected by these two diseases is substantial, and their effects, as evidenced by Caroline, can be devastating. Fortunately, some progress is being made, but the progress must happen more quickly.

A closely related implication involves medical insurance. It is imperative that insurance carriers recognize Lyme disease and other environmentally acquired illnesses and provide adequate coverage for them. At present, insurance companies penalize doctors for diagnosing complex illnesses that require treatments the insurance company doesn't cover. Even if the patient has the resources to cover specialized out-of-pocket treatments, doctors that take insurance avoid treatments the insurance companies categorize as unnecessary or experimental, even when researchers have proven it safe and effective. Furthermore, as Caroline indicates, ERISA stands as a significant barrier for some employees to receive adequate insurance coverage. There must be a review of this act and its potential effects on hundreds of thousands of employees.

Finally, we do fully support health insurance and adequate health care for all. We appreciate the role that the Affordable Care Act has played in increasing health-care coverage for millions of additional Americans, and we urge our elected officials to identify ways to add even more of our fellow citizens to the rolls of those covered. In short, no one should be bankrupted to pay for medical care.

Lyme, Mold, Environmentally Acquired Illness, and Mental Illness

As Caroline explains,

> Some of the most visible symptoms of Lyme and mold illness look a great deal like mental illness—fatigue, malaise, perseverating thoughts, extreme mood swings, panic, anxiety, depression, and rage. However, these symptoms have a well-defined, physiological source—they are the result of brain swelling and systemic inflammation. So, this begs the question: How many cases of mental illness are actually the result of a treatable, underlying medical condition? All too often, doctors jump straight to "depression" and the conversation ends there.

Caroline goes on to say that Harvard-trained, board-certified psychiatrist Mary Ackerley became a board-certified integrative physician, which allows her to explore the physiological source of her patients' symptoms and to provide more meaningful care that actually addresses root causes. She developed a practice that evaluated the factors impacting brain health, including neurotransmitters, hormone imbalances, immune deficiency, genetic mutations, and hidden infections such as Lyme and mold illness. Now, in addition to her busy practice, Dr. Ackerley serves as vice president of the medical nonprofit International Society of Environmentally Acquired Illness. The members of the society are conducting the research needed to bring mold illness and other environmentally acquired illness into mainstream medicine.

Advocates for Those with Cognitive Issues

According to Caroline,

> I cannot explain the complexity of managing all of these different systems. Even when I've stated that I had cognitive and memory issues and needed help completing a form, being reminded of a requirement, or understanding the implications of a decision, the response was tepid at best. I've been penalized for decisions I made during this ordeal, because I didn't fully understand the requirement or downstream impact. Even though I stated my limitations clearly, no one with special training was assigned to me, and no responsibility was taken by the other party for their failure to provide adequate explanation or support for my established disability. I was never offered an accommodation, or caseworker to help me, even when working with government agencies.

Somehow, in the case of persons with reduced cognitive capacity, we must create a better system of personal advocates, those individuals who will be available to assist in cases of medical and/or housing issues. This is a central concern in the disability community, especially for those with cognitive and developmental disabilities, but we must expand the reach of that community to include people with chronic illnesses that have affected their cognitive ability. As Caroline indicates, private advocates often charge more than $100 per hour to "ask the right questions, anticipate pitfalls, and stay current with deadlines and requirements." Many simply cannot afford this kind of assistance. As a consequence, this role often falls to a family member, neighbor, or friend who then becomes a kind of caregiver, frequently without the necessary expertise or skills. We must create a broader cadre of persons with the expertise and skills necessary to assist individuals like Caroline.

Housing and Poverty

As we described earlier, low-rent, affordable, and attainable housing is virtually nonexistent for many in cities, towns, suburbs, and rural areas across the country. The deficit in such units for all those paying more than 30 percent of their income for housing is increasing every year; it is now almost 8 million units nationally, and it is especially hard to find such units in Caroline's home state. This becomes even more problematic for those who are disabled and cannot work at all, like Caroline. As she states,

> The "poverty line" also hasn't scaled with housing prices. Even if I get Social Security disability, the income threshold is so low that even in "affordable housing," I'd spend at least 50 percent of my meager $1,500 per month on housing—with barely anything left over to cover the other basics of utilities, car insurance, gasoline, healthy food, or health care. . . . If I gross more than $1,200 per month, I lose government assistance. But how can I live on $1,000 net a month?

She goes on to say,

> That I am expected to survive on $398 per month in public assistance until my disability can be awarded is insane. I cannot eat and cover basics like car insurance or repairs (on a twenty-year old car), a phone bill, clothing, toiletries, or laundry detergent—and I'm the lucky one. Many without homes don't have the medical documentation to prove their disability or jump through the incredible hoops required to maintain public assistance. Do we only deserve to thrive if we have a spouse, or children? Or loving, affluent parents? Or a church community? Or significant financial resources?

According to a 2015 study by the Economic Policy Institute (EPI), a single person living in Denver can maintain "a modest, but adequate standard of living" if they make $28,829 per year. However, the EPI budget allocated $600 a month for housing and utilities. The poverty level for a single adult without children is around

$1,005 per month, gross (Wissman, 2017). Rusch, in the *Denver Post* (2016), reported the average cost of a one-bedroom apartment in Denver is $1,390 a month.

The poverty level is too low to effectively support life, and the Denver example is repeated in virtually every case across the country. If the intent is to sustain life in times of crisis, the poverty level should be set closer to the actual cost of living. In short, there must be a substantial readjustment in determining poverty levels that includes accurate data about the cost of housing, as $600 a month for housing and utilities is far too little to afford any type of housing in most urban areas.

Georgescu, in his compelling book, *Capitalists Arise!* (2017), argued that private corporations are being held hostage by their stockholders and that the push for short-term profits is replacing the much-needed investment in the corporations' employees and the all-important R&D function. He argued convincingly that corporations should pay their workers more and give them more say in how the business is being conducted. He also argued for a much greater investment in research and development, in part as a way to increase overall employment and to improve the quality of products and services. These are intriguing ideas.

Another increasingly considered concept is a universal basic income. People on both sides of the political and economic aisle are advocating such an approach. Typically, advocates promote either an annual income amount or a monthly stipend for everyone. These benefits would replace existing benefit programs, such as Social Security, SSI and SSDI, TANF, SNAP, WIC, EITC, and many others. Many advocates argue that by moving to such a system, much of the confusion about benefits would be eliminated, federal management of the system would be vastly simplified, the problem of eligible recipients not receiving benefits would be eliminated, and this benefit would lift millions of people out of poverty.

There can be no doubt that the implementation of any of these systemic changes will have a significant impact on our national budget. However, in the interest of increasing revenue and reducing economic inequality, here are a few suggestions for consideration.

First, let's eliminate or at least reduce the mortgage interest deduction (MID). The MID is one of the most regressive tax instruments currently in the US tax code; it provides a benefit to only those households that are wealthy enough to own their own homes and to itemize their tax deductions. Recent changes in the tax code have provided a bit of relief by increasing the standard deduction, but elimination of the MID would go much further in producing revenue and creating greater equality.

Another way to think about this is the possibility of reversing the regressive elements of existing housing subsidies. Instead of the mortgage interest deduction that benefits wealthy homeowners, perhaps we should create tax benefits for housing renters, especially low-income renters. There currently exists the Earned Income Tax Credit, but this focuses on income. Suppose, instead, we provide a tax credit to low-income renters whose overall revenue stream fell below some percentage of the poverty level. Admittedly, the American Dream includes "owning your own home," and home ownership is the most frequent way in which families develop assets through increasing equity; however, this whole system favors those who can afford to buy a home. Shouldn't we be thinking about ways to provide increased subsidies for those who can only afford to rent their homes?

In light of the recent tax code changes, it is imperative that there be a substantial overhaul of the entire tax code. Despite minimal benefits for lower-middle- and middle-class taxpayers, the vast majority of the benefits accrue to the wealthy. This must be corrected.

Finally, another approach toward greater equity can be achieved through means testing major benefit programs. This should apply to Social Security, Medicare, and the Universal Basic Income. There is no reason, from an equity standpoint, why wealthy Americans should get substantial economic benefits from the federal government. Therefore, we would argue that, if a household is over a certain level of income, it should not receive Social Security or a basic income payment and it should pay for all its medical care. At the very least, these types of benefit amounts should be graduated depending on income, much the way federal income tax is calculated. We would argue that the same framework should be applied to corporations. Large, multinational corporations that are raking in billions of dollars of annual profit should be paying their fair share of taxes.

Better Building Standards

Mold infestation and water damage are endemic conditions in many of our buildings across the country, especially in multiunit buildings such as public housing and facilities that accept housing vouchers. In light of the abortive attempts by Caroline to find a housing unit free of mold, it is imperative that local, state, and federal housing authorities and private landlords make a substantially greater effort to assess the livability of units under their auspices. Simply applying a sponge with water and bleach as an antidote to mold, as was suggested in Caroline's experience in one unit, is totally unsatisfactory. Meaningful mold assessment and remediation are a humane response to renting a unit to someone with an environmentally acquired illness, and, in the long run, it is a much cheaper option than being the negligent landlord at the wrong end of a lawsuit.

The Support of Community

Incredible though it may be, in her story, Caroline states that she is happier now than she has ever been, more accepting of her situation, more at peace with herself and with her life. As she indicates, "When things are at their worst, my default response is joy and loving kindness. I love deeply and fully just because it feels good." In light of her situation, how can this be? How can anyone be happier now, yet be faced with the obstacles she has to face?

In short, the answer is that she has an indomitable spirit that has been fueled and reinforced by strong and reliable support. Her Lyme support group has been invaluable to her, and she can rely on members of that group to be helpful with suggestions, some financial help, good wishes, and a strong caring ethos that surrounds her. She can also rely on other caring individuals who have listened to her, believed her story, provided access to other resources, and whose interest in her and her story has been supportive to her. As she states in one part of her story, a colleague of hers who has been through much the same set of events as she has indicated to her that, without friends and lots of help, they would have committed suicide. Caroline strongly believes that she herself would have followed this path without her caring community, her friends, her support group. After all, this is what community, natural supports, and friends are all about. They saved her, making her feel like part of a community, just as others like them were instrumental for most of our other contributors.

11

Toward Eradicating Homelessness

Despite the billions of dollars spent by federal, state, and local governments, by private charities, and by concerned citizens; despite the hundreds of millions of paid and volunteer person-hours; and despite the millions of words uttered and published imploring us to do better, the number of persons experiencing homelessness has not changed significantly in the last several decades. In fact, the overall numbers actually increased between 2016 and 2017 (US Department of Housing and Urban Development, 2017a). While we have made progress in reducing veteran homelessness nationally and chronic homelessness in some locales, overall numbers remain stubbornly high.

Lessons from the Contributors

Although each story is different, there are common themes in how our contributors became homeless. One of these themes is trauma, especially the trauma caused by family dysfunction, as was the case with Barb, Tim, Tiffany, Blizzard, and James, although each suffered the consequences of the family's issues at different stages in their lives. Michelle and Caroline became homeless through system errors: Michelle due to an administrative error regarding her college financial aid, Caroline through medical failure to properly diagnose her illnesses. Leanne was the victim of a major national economic down-turn, a series of events that has had a major impact on thousands of families across the county. Finally, Marie's parents were unable to get the legal help they needed, which had a significant impact on the family's housing circumstances for years.

As we have discussed at the ends of the chapters, the stories suggest a number of important implications. From the individual stories of each contributor, there are numerous macro and micro implications for the field. Barb's journey explores the need for a safe, stable home and the effects of adverse childhood experiences and childhood trauma. Her experiences with homelessness as a child, like many others, left long-term ramifications even into adulthood. She also explores the shame that so many of those living without a place to call home struggle with, affecting their ability to function and cope.

Tim's journey provides insight into the type of family dysfunction behind the astonishing number of homeless youth in this country who are without the support of a parent or guardian. Family dysfunction requires a holistic approach, such as family resource centers, which focus on supporting families to become healthy and self-sufficient. As Tim states, family resource centers "bring together services and activities that educate, develop skills, and promote positive family interactions to improve outcomes for both families and communities. This increases the capacity of families to be resilient, healthy, and involved members of their community." He goes on to add, "This approach of involving families in problem solving, while at the same time developing skills, abilities, and talents, works to invest in and support healthy and functioning families and communities."

Marie's journey, a story of family homelessness precipitated by the convergence of multiple underlying circumstances, sets the stage to explore several macro implications, many of which relate directly to the deficit in affordable housing and the underlying issue of economic inequality. Creating robust data systems that collect and track the impact of efforts to end homelessness and implementing an efficient coordinated entry system in conjunction with evidence-based housing practices are important steps in ending homelessness. Additionally, Marie's chapter demonstrates how even minor criminal justice involvement can impact an individual or family's ability to maintain housing. Lastly, her story provides insight into the experience of millions of families in our country caught in the in-between, unable to afford a home of their own, yet able to sustain temporary living situations such as long-term motels; her journey suggests the need to expand options and support for these families.

The need for placements that provide alternatives to foster care is a strong implication of Tiffany's journey, along with the necessity of child welfare reform overall. Additionally, Tiffany's chapter explores the importance of educational institutions in the lives of students experiencing homelessness, from elementary and secondary schools all the way to the college level, either through individual teachers or through organizational programs aimed at providing school stability such as McKinney-Vento, as seen in Marie's journey, or the TRIO program seeking to support first-generation college students in Tiffany's journey. Consequently, educational institutions at all levels must be more aware of who among their students is experiencing homelessness, how those students can be assisted even more than they currently are, and how to receive the adequate funding and resources to do so.

Similar to Tiffany's journey, Blizzard's provides further insight into additional gaps in child welfare and what should be done to address them. Perhaps most striking is the need to support youth as they transition out of care, providing them access to services until the age of maturation, and allowing them to reenter care as needed. His story also explores the difficulties of life on the streets and the consequences of criminalizing homelessness, demonstrating how this system can become a revolving door for so many of our nation's youth, one that requires significant reform.

Leanne's journey uncovers how an individual who has done everything right can be the victim of an economic downturn and a crumbling support network. She, a veteran with an education and strong will to succeed, had her world turned upside down during the Great Recession, demonstrating the negative outcomes of turbulent economic times. A hard look at employment, wages, and strengthening prevention strategies is necessary.

In Chapter 8, Michelle shares her journey of racial bias and a service industry modeled after the assembly line. A simple clerical error led to a grandmother and veteran with an established work history finding herself without a place to call home, resulting in months of struggle with a system not equipped to support her as she sought to finish her education. She endured racial bias and outright employment discrimination, and was forced to miss classes due to the strict rules of her housing provider. Her experiences highlight the issues of race and the need for more flexible, client-centered services that support the specific needs of each person, instead of presenting yet another set of barriers, especially for those actively pursuing a path toward self-sufficiency.

Adequate legal representation is a need identified in several chapters and highlighted in James's. Forced into a familial court battle, without access to adequate legal counsel, James found himself without a place to live after caring for his ailing mother. He, like so many others, was the victim of a complicated judicial system, and better and more extensive legal assistance would have helped James immeasurably, suggesting the strong need for increased legal aid for those experiencing homelessness, including those who are facing evictions.

Caroline's journey indicates how a chronic medical condition obliterated her financial security, a situation facing millions of Americans each year. From her story we see the need for significant reform to our existing health-care system. Both the medical profession and medical insurance companies must become more familiar with a variety of diseases not currently covered by insurance, thereby eliminating the frequent misdiagnosis of mental illness, the need for reform of ERISA, and the adoption of better building standards.

Throughout the book, there are some implications and themes that arise in all of the contributors' stories. One of them can best be described with one word: bandwidth. (For an examination of this concept, see Mullainathan and Shafir, 2013.) These nine sets of experiences clearly demonstrate that the condition of homelessness creates immense pressure on individuals to cope, forcing them to focus their energy and brain power on getting through each day; this reduces their ability to plan systematically for the future. Service providers must take that into consideration when working with individuals and families without homes.

One of the most common characteristics among those experiencing homelessness, and a significant factor in reducing bandwidth, is the trauma that they have experienced: the trauma of not having a home; the trauma of living on the streets, in cars, in rundown motels, or in vastly overcrowded and unhealthy shelters; the trauma of rejection and disdain; the trauma of untreated alcohol and/or substance abuse; the trauma of mental illness; the trauma of dysfunctional family relationships; the trauma of domestic and/or other violence; and the trauma of harassment. Therefore, service providers across the board need to be cognizant that homelessness is indeed traumatic, robbing individuals and families of intellectual, emotional, and psychological energy. Every service provider must become steeped in trauma-informed care, and every interaction with a person experiencing homelessness must start from that premise.

Finally, perhaps the biggest takeaway from our nine stories is what we call the need for human capital. The homelessness of all our contributors was interrupted and altered by one or more caring individuals, people who took the time to listen, to understand, to appreciate the gifts that each of our contributors had. In some cases it was a parent, in other cases it was a teacher or a counselor, but in every case, it was someone who cared. James had a network of people who could be of help to him. Marie, Tiffany, Leanne, and Caroline became part of a group of individuals who served as a kind of community of like-minded spirits. While the macro implications discussed throughout this book are of incredible importance, human capital was also a major factor that each of the contributors identified as instrumental in their exiting homelessness.

Systemic Changes

The field of social work provides one useful way of thinking about homelessness and how to address it. It distinguishes between micro social work and macro social work. In the micro arena, as Michael Reisch (2014) indicated, the focus is on dealing with individuals, couples, families, and groups. In contrast, macro social work "pushes the boundaries of the profession by fostering a 'big picture' perspective that enables social workers and society as a whole to analyze people's issues 'outside the box' and focus on the prevention of problems, not their amelioration" (Reisch, 2014, p. 6). "Its goal is to 'bring about *planned change* in . . . systems" (Netting et al., 2011, cited in Reisch, 2014, p. 5; emphasis in Netting). However, as Reisch pointed out, both threads of the work are guided by a strong social justice theme.

This important distinction between micro and macro approaches extends beyond social work. In fact, this distinction can be employed in many areas of our society and is endemic to much of the social policy research and practice that have been carried out in this country for decades. The micro approach certainly represents much of what we as a nation have done over the last forty years to address homelessness. By and large, service providers have focused their attention on providing a response to the individual needs of persons and families, trying to assist them in improving their situations, ameliorating their circumstances. Although there are a number of national organizations that are trying to create changes in systems, such as the National Low Income Housing Coalition, the National Law Center on Homelessness and Poverty, the National Alliance to End Homelessness, among others, the vast majority of work has been at a micro level. In fact, as Reisch (2014), Rothman (2013), and

George (2018) point out, schools of social work provide few curricular offerings to train their students in creating systemic change. We argue that this characteristic is common to many undergraduate and graduate institutions of higher learning.

Throughout this book, we have tried to be mindful of both micro and macro approaches to the issue of homelessness. There is certainly a major need to ameliorate the conditions of all those experiencing homelessness, as our nine contributors can attest. The existing panoply of service providers needs to continue to address the needs of individuals and families, without question. However, all of the micro efforts will have little impact on the overall homelessness issue unless there are major changes in our social and economic systems.

A thorough examination of all these is beyond the scope of this book, but we have identified some possible changes throughout the book, including more low-income housing; a system for better legal representation; higher wages and better jobs; changes in the tax system; improved discharge planning; changes in the foster care and juvenile care systems; better health care and health insurance systems; an improved unemployment insurance system; and an expansion of the system of family resource centers, including a 2Gen approach.

A Revised Emphasis

There is no question that more housing and more wraparound services are needed (see, for example, various chapters in Burnes & DiLeo, 2016; National Low Income Housing Coalition, 2018a). We know the need, and we have good program models that help us provide the tools for people to move into housing and services. However, as our contributors suggest, that is not enough. Besides major systemic changes, it is imperative that we become more sensitive to the needs of those experiencing homelessness on a micro level. Here we suggest a few ways of thinking about that.

Adopting an Equipping Model

The common philosophical approach of those providing services to people without homes is based on a medical or "treatment" model. According to this philosophy, there is something to be treated, and service providers are there to cure it. Much as the medical profession is trained to solve the medical problems of its patients, many homelessness service providers are similarly trained to solve the problems of its clients. It is no wonder that many service providers are called case managers or clinicians.

However, as we have tried to argue throughout this book, and as our contributors have demonstrated repeatedly, many persons experiencing homelessness are there through no fault of their own. Dysfunctional parents, fiscal crises such as the banking chaos of the late 2000s, medical emergencies and poorly treated diseases, corporate downsizing, inadequate housing opportunities, low wages, and so forth have forced most of our contributors and the majority of those experiencing homelessness out of a home. At one point, our argument was that we should call for an empowerment model, empowering people to take charge of their own lives.

However, Tiffany put the lie to this concept when she said that she didn't need power; she had the power. What she needed was the tools. Thanks to her, we now call it the "equipping model," that is, we need to equip people experiencing homelessness with the tools they need to secure and maintain permanent housing and to obtain the other services they may need. There is an old axiom, "Give a man a fish; he eats for a day. Teach a man to fish, he eats for a lifetime." We would add, "Yes, that's fine, but sometimes the man needs a fishing pole and bait." That is what the equipping model is all about. Or, as the director of a local Jewish Family and Children's Services center wrote in a recent op-ed piece, "The real benefit is giving people the tools they need to be self-sufficient" (Hines, 2018, p. 4D). To put it another way, pulling yourself up by your bootstraps is only possible if you have boots.

From Individual to Community

One of the significant characteristics of homeless services across the United States is their primary focus on the individual, a clinical approach to amelioration. A case manager is assigned to an individual, who then tries to identify an individual unit of housing and individual services as needed for the individual client. Most agencies do little to create nonprofessional networks of support or to help the client develop participation in a community.

Unfortunate though that may be, it is very much in keeping with the spirit of American culture—everyone out for himself or herself, the Horatio Alger heroic effort to be an important and self-sufficient individual. Despite such writings as *Habits of the Heart* (Bellah, Madsen, Sullivan, & Tipton, 1985), *Democracy in America* (de Tocqueville, 1961), and others, in which authors have described the universal desire for a greater sense of community, we continue to model behavior that is focused on the individual.

Need for Community

The contributors of the nine stories in this book identify the importance of caring individuals, the value of networks of support, and the centrality of a sense of community, all of which were instrumental in helping them through their homelessness. In some cases, schoolteachers were most significant; in other cases, there were small groups of like-minded people such as JROTC, TRIO, and the Lyme disease support group; in still other cases, there was a parent or other family member who formed the glue for successfully escaping homelessness. However, in every case, there was a person or a group of people who were instrumental in helping our contributors escape the ravages of homelessness.

This is not to say that housing and wraparound services are not important. Of course they are. Also important are the needed changes in aspects of the social and economic system that create homelessness, such as increased minimum wages, increased availability of low-income housing, and improved health care. One might describe it this way: Housing assistance and assorted services are critically important for getting many folks off the streets, out of shelters, out of transitional housing, out of motels, and out of doubled-up situations, and into some type of more permanent housing and services. However, the human resources—the caring individuals, the networks of support, and the community—can also be critical for helping some people gain access to their own homes, and for keeping people in their housing and helping them lead more stable, self-sufficient, and satisfying lives.

Simply providing most people currently experiencing homelessness or those on the very edge of becoming homeless with a network of support will not automatically eliminate homelessness for them. Yes, they need housing and, in many cases, other kinds of services. However, we argue, eventually, as they get into housing situations, they will need to rely on natural support systems beyond professional service providers.

Most of us have an important network of support that we can call on in times of crisis and emergency. Family members, friends, neighbors, church members, and club members are all potential sources of support in such times. These network supports are people one can call on at 2:00 a.m. in times of crisis. For most people experiencing homelessness, they can't call the caseworker or service provider because those professional helpers are not available at that time of the morning. Thus, having someone to contact is critical.

For most people experiencing homelessness, such networks of support are nonexistent. They either never had them, or they used them up by placing too many demands on them. A recent report by SPARC described yet another situation that the authors called *network impoverishment*, where the networks were too poor to be able to provide any real support, especially financial support (Olivet et al., 2018) and were, therefore, not of much help.

In short, people experiencing homelessness need many resources like housing, health and behavioral health care services, assistance with job training and job placement, and trauma-informed care, but they also need human resources, social capital, caring individuals, networks of support, and community. These resources are essential for people to avoid entering homelessness or to escape homelessness if they are already there.

To illustrate the need for a network and community, a landlord recruiter described the following story. She had worked long hours to persuade a certain landlord to allow an individual who had been living in a shelter to rent an apartment. On the lease-up and move-in day, this person, rather than sleeping in his new apartment, returned to the shelter because that's where his friends, his community, were (C. Blair, personal communication, October 4, 2018).

A recent study about health-care struggles for persons experiencing homelessness stated, "Others lack positive social networks that support them in their health goals" (Hardee, Sanford, & Burnes, 2019, p. 77). The authors added, "Homeless persons lacking meaningful relationships should be provided resources to find social support, including peers, groups, or day programs. This network will give them people to contact, whether in emergencies or situations requiring guidance. The caring community also allows them to overcome social isolation" (Hardee et al., 2019, p. 79).

Creating Networks and Community

What is meant by *community*? Psychologists David W. McMillan and David M. Chavis outlined four basic elements of community in a 1986 article titled "Sense of Community: A Definition and Theory." Those were membership, or "the feeling of belonging"; influence, or the "sense of mattering, of making a difference to a group"; reinforcement, or "the feeling that members' needs will be met"; and shared emotional connection, or the "belief that members have shared and will share history, common places, time together and similar experiences" (quoted in Chocano, 2018, p. 14). McMillan and Chavis also cited an important distinction between two types of community that have long coexisted. One is geographical—neighborhood, town, city—and the other is "relational," concerned with the interconnections among people.

As Chocano (2018) suggested, there are many definitions of community. Throughout this book, our contributors and the two of us as coauthors have used the concept of community in many of the ways highlighted by McMillan and Chavis. For most of our contributors, their community was defined geographically; however, they all focused on the relational aspect of their networks of support, their community. These communities included caring individuals, small groups that provided support, and others.

There is another important dimension of community that is often overlooked. As Matt Mollica said recently, "Community is about choice" (M. Mollica & D. Witsky, personal communication, May 31, 2018). People choose to be in community with people they know and like, people with whom they share one or another of the four elements of community that McMillan and Chavis outlined above. Unfortunately, in the world of homelessness services, there are usually very few real choices that people experiencing homelessness can make. They are told which housing unit to go to and which services they need. Even with Housing Choice vouchers, one of the several types of housing subsidies currently available, there are usually so few units from which to choose, that a person experiencing homelessness has virtually no "choice" in the type of housing he or she can go into or in the neighborhood in which the housing unit is located. For example, in a recent study conducted by the Burnes Center (2018) in Adams County, a Denver suburb, the local housing authority indicated that they hand out about 1,400 housing vouchers each year, and 60 percent are returned unused because no units were available, and some landlords refused to let the voucher holder rent in their buildings. So, where's the choice for those individuals and families?

This lack of choice wherein service providers make decisions about where people live leads frequently to a resegregation of low-income residents, often already segregated by race and gender. Because of negative stereotypes, ignorance regarding people who are experiencing homelessness, and a lack of understanding of the systemic forces that usually cause homelessness, potential neighbors often object strenuously to siting service facilities in middle-class neighborhoods. Thus, the attitude of "not in my backyard," (NIMBY) rears its ugly head.

Networks of Support and the
Dual Definitions of Homelessness

As we pointed out in Chapter 1, there are two major definitions of homelessness at the federal level. HUD's definition is fairly narrow and specifically excludes most individuals, families, and children who are doubled up, couch surfing with relatives, friends, or neighbors. The definition used by the US Department of Education is much broader and includes all these persons. As we indicated in Chapter 1, the difference between the definitions creates close to a fivefold difference in the overall number of persons considered to be experiencing homelessness. We also have indicated that in Marie's case, her sleeping in doubled-up situations meant that she and her family were not eligible for HUD-funded services.

In a recent discussion, a senior housing official stated, "Families that are using their networks [i.e., couch surfing] are being penalized by HUD for doing just that" (B. Fisher, personal communication, April 11, 2019). The implication of HUD's refusal to include persons who are couch surfing for an extended period of time is that long-term use of a network means that the individual or family is appropriately housed and not in need of their own housing, despite the often deleterious effects of such housing circumstances on adults and especially children.

Examples of Creating Communities

Despite the unfortunate consequences of much of what we do in the name of addressing homelessness, there are some encouraging examples of efforts to create networks and community. Miracle Messages is one example of the effort to build networks. As the director of Miracle Messages, Kevin Adler, said,

> I believe part of the problem is that we have been looking at the problem all wrong. When a person becomes homeless, they lose a lot more than just their physical housing. Often, they lose touch with their families and friends, too. Over time, this social disconnectedness has all sorts of negative impacts on a person's sense of self-esteem and possibility, making it more difficult for

them to form relationships, accept help, realize goals, maintain their well-being, and (yes) even find stable housing.

The loss of one's social support system and sense of belonging—the "social home," as we have come to call it at Miracle Messages—is rarely addressed by homeless service providers. But with an estimated minimum of 35% of home-lessness caused by what can be termed "relational brokenness" (divorce or separation, an argument with a family member who asked them to leave, domestic violence), and potentially a major contributing factor in cases of job loss, substance abuse, incar-ceration, and mental and physical health outcomes, the loss of one's social home is a primary concern of people actually living on the streets.

Most homeless service providers focus on the base of Maslow's hierarchy of needs: food, water, shelter, clothing, hygiene. These basic needs are essential to human survival. But we humans are complex. We also need to feel a sense of belonging, self-esteem, and love. These social supports are crucial for preventing—and exiting—homelessness, as evidenced by the ample research from studies of youth homeless-ness (K. Adler, personal communication, January 15, 2018). The focus of Miracle Messages, originally founded in San Francisco, is the cre-ation of audio and/or video messages by unsheltered persons to long-lost family members and friends, thus creating an opportunity for fam-ily reunification using the tools of the digital age. As Adler stated,

> Over the past three years, Miracle Messages has helped over 100 people experiencing homelessness reunite with their loved ones, all through short video messages (and recently, audio messages via our client hotline, 1-800-MISS-YOU), social media, and local volunteers. My team and I are on a mission to end homelessness by rebuilding social support systems, one conversation at a time. We envision a world where everyone is nurtured by a social sup-port system and sense of belonging—a *social home*—whether or not they currently have physical housing. Our goal is to reunite 10,000 people with their loved ones by 2023 and, in the process, build nurturing relationships between our homeless neighbors and the rest of us as a society, and tell those stories well. We are a movement to end relational poverty on our streets.

Kevin Adler's Miracle Messages isn't the only program that is focusing on human resources, support networks, and community by leveraging technology for those experiencing homelessness. Another unique model utilizing the tools of the digital age to create networks of support is Purposity, a nonprofit technology platform originally created to support students identified as homeless in public schools. Through storytelling, the app builds awareness in local communities on the needs of those experiencing homelessness and poverty. Its basic premise is that while no one can do everything, everyone can do something. The app allows users to meet needs from their phone in their local community, creating an online network of support for essential resources while giving community members a tangible action step to combat large social issues such as homelessness.

The recent focus on peer support and peer navigators is another way in which the country is trying to help develop networks of support. With increased attention to involving persons with lived experience, the addition of those persons as quasi–case managers and members of support teams is a natural extension.

However, as an experienced trainer reported recently, there is an assumption that folks who have experienced homelessness in the past know how to provide support to others and are already experts in working with others. "Many of them really don't know how to provide the kind of support that people need, and they almost certainly don't have training in trauma-informed care" (Y. Perret, personal communication, April 24, 2019). She suggested the need for a real training program for peer support staff and peer navigators.

More traditional methods can also be employed to build these critical networks of support. Dr. Daniel Brisson and his colleagues at the Burnes Center on Poverty and Homelessness in Denver have developed a twelve-week educational training program for residents in low-income communities that provides residents and their children with the tools they need to be more strongly connected to the schools their children attend and to develop a greater sense of social and community cohesion. The program, Your Family, Your Neighborhood, is now in its third year, and Dr. Brisson refers to it as "intervention research," as in, he is introducing this pilot program into neighborhoods in Denver and is also evaluating its impact on both the low-income families and those neighborhoods.

In Ocean County, New Jersey, James Abro has worked to create a permanent emergency housing facility for people experiencing homelessness. His dream is to develop an emergency shelter for those who are currently living on the streets of Asbury Park and in the woods of Toms River. Although there will be services at the shelter for individuals, one of Abro's primary goals is to create networks of support among the residents at the shelter so that individuals will have people to rely on in the future in case of emergencies.

The burgeoning movement toward the creation of tent cities and tiny-home villages is another example of an effort to create networks and community in temporary or transitional housing situations. We are not suggesting that these types of living situations are a solution to homelessness, rather that they serve as a very temporary form of transitional housing and can provide a sense of community during this transitional situation. The Right to Dream Too in the middle of downtown Portland, Oregon, is one such example. This tent city houses overnight sleeping space for about forty men, about fifteen women, couples, and people with pets. It also has space for about twenty individual tents that house single people or couples. There is a small kitchen-like area, an office tent with computers, portable restrooms, and running water and electricity. The residents have also created an extensive list of rules of behavior that govern activity in the tent city. During a recent tour, it was clear that everyone knew each other and that there was truly a sense of community; people had each other's backs.

The Beloved Community Village (BCV) in Denver is another such example. Created in July 2017, BCV houses fourteen people at present in eleven tiny homes. Each unit has access to some electricity; there are portable restrooms on the grounds; there is a separate building with sinks, running water, and showers; and there is a communal cooking, eating, and meeting area. In its evaluation report on this pilot project, the Burnes Center on Poverty and Homelessness indicated that, over the first eight months of its existence, BCV in fact created an intentional community, although that was never an explicit goal of the project. The report stated that there was a strong sense that BCV provided an otherwise nonexistent support system to many of the residents and a valued opportunity to be part of something larger than themselves. These support networks were described as comprising other BCV residents as well as the surrounding neighborhood and greater BCV community, including members of the Colorado Village Collaborative, Denver Homeless Out Loud, Bayaud Enterprises, and others. The diversity represented not only by BCV residents but also by members of the broader BCV community was cited as a positive aspect of the experience.

Residents of the program reported the following feedback regarding the program: "We hang out together and look out for each other. We love our outside community too; they are very good to us!" "It's good reassurance that you're part of something" (Burnes Center on Poverty and Homelessness, 2018, p. 22).

Other cities have also created tent cities and tiny-home villages in an effort to provide temporary housing for those experiencing homelessness. Here again, we are not suggesting that these should in any way be a solution to long-term housing, but rather that if these types of short-term solutions are necessary, they should be safe places in which to temporarily reside while being connected to permanent housing. In Seattle, for example, there are six formally sanctioned encampments, most of which have a combination of tent homes and tiny homes. In each encampment, there are significant efforts under way to create community. The same holds true for the tent city in Eugene, Oregon. For an excellent review of tent cities and tiny-home villages, including a set of recommendations on how to develop such housing and community situations, see *Tent City Urbanism* (Heben, 2014). Although there are various community living environments, the ones identified above are specifically for those individuals and families that are experiencing homelessness, and one of their main functions is to develop a sense of community.

A longtime example of community building is the national Oxford House program. Initiated in 1975, Oxford Houses are intended as a community living situation for men or women in recovery from alcoholism and/or drug addiction. An average of eight men or women rent space in a large single-family dwelling and provide dedicated support for each other's ongoing sobriety and recovery; the houses range in size from six to sixteen individuals. In the Oxford House International 2017 Annual Report, the authors indicated that there are 18,025 recovery beds in 2,287 such houses located in 481 cities in forty-four states in the United States. Since the program's outset forty-three years ago, over 400,000 people have lived in Oxford Houses across the country. Of the 2017 residents, almost 70 percent were experiencing homelessness at the time they became residents of an Oxford House. A significant feature of the Oxford Houses is that participants choose to be there. If a resident relapses, he or she is asked to leave, but in most cases is encouraged to return when he or she is ready to continue the road to recovery (Oxford House, 2018).

The success of the Oxford House movement offers an important lesson. Smaller groupings of people may facilitate a greater sense of community than larger congregate settings for certain populations of those experiencing homelessness. Tiny-home villages, small sanctioned encampments, Oxford House–type facilities, and smaller permanent and permanent supported housing buildings provide an opportunity to build communities of support that last.

In Kansas City, Kansas, Kerry Wrenick and colleagues developed Impact Wednesday, a program that has two basic purposes. One day a week, various service agencies and other community organizations come together to provide services for schoolchildren experiencing homelessness in that school district. At other times, a community hub has been created for parents and children to feel welcome and to develop into a community group. As Wrenick explained, "Most of these families have had very negative experiences with schools, and this gets transferred to their children. What we are trying to do is to make their experiences more positive, and we promise to work with the families to make sure they secure long-term housing while maintaining their sense of community" (K. Wrenick, personal communication, May 22, 2018).

In Australia,

Doorway is an innovative three-year pilot program funded by the Victorian Department of Health (DoH) and implemented by Mental Illness Fellowship Victoria (MI Fellowship) that crosses traditional program boundaries of mental health, housing and economic participation. Doorway is designed to enhance the capacity of individuals with a serious mental illness (SMI) *who are homeless or at risk of homelessness* to lead independent, healthy and meaningful lives in housing and communities *of their choice. The program explicitly focuses on addressing social isolation and increasing client confidence and choice— both elements often missing from traditional approaches to housing and recovery.*

The Doorway model supports participants to choose, access and sustain their own private rental accommodation by subsidizing participants' rental payments where required and building their independent living and tenancy management skills. Participants in the Doorway pilot are empowered to self-direct their support needs by designing and managing their own integrated support teams. These teams are comprised of core elements—such as family members, friends and AMHS (Area Mental Health Services) case managers—and flexible elements which may include workers from employment and other health support services. Doorway also supports participants to develop and/or extend their *informal social supports*, through an intentional approach to developing their *natural support networks*. The relationships between participants and their integrated teams and natural support networks are initially established, nurtured and mediated by Doorway's Housing and Recovery Workers (H&RWs). (Nous Group, 2014, p. 5; emphasis added)

Other examples of efforts to build networks of support and community for those experiencing homelessness exist. Some agencies provide opportunities for group activities. Various clubs provide similar types of opportunities. Tenant councils in subsidized housing facilities offer another way of developing community. In short, if attention is paid to creating the kinds of human resources that people experiencing homelessness want and need, a variety of ways exist for providing them.

Formalizing Support Networks

Interestingly, there are two excellent models for building formalized networks of support and community from other disciplines. The arena of developmental disabilities has created a whole movement around developing circles of support. This is not to suggest that homelessness is like a disability, but rather that the idea of circles of support can be useful in creating larger, more robust networks. Based on the writings of John McKnight and Mike Green and work initiated in Canada, circles of support have become a major focus among groups that work with people with developmental disabilities. Initiated by the question, "What happens to the individual with a developmental disability after the parents are gone?" and a strong desire not to rely too heavily on professional caregivers, circles often focus on creating plans for the focus person. With the help of circle members—family members, friends, and persons of similar interests to the focus person—the focus person identifies hopes and dreams for the future, the types of resources he or she needs, and a series of action steps that need to be taken, allowing for choice and self-determination. Circle members pledge to assist as needed and to continue to meet regularly with the focus person to provide support in the process of realizing hopes and dreams. In this way, a formal, dedicated support network is created to assist in equipping the individual in pursuing his or her chosen path.

Another prime example of a formalized structure to build a network of support is the model utilized by organizations such as Alcoholics Anonymous or Narcotics Anonymous. Again, this is *not* to suggest that homelessness is like an addiction; it is simply to offer a model of how networks of support might be structured. In these models, there are three key features that are particularly relevant. One is sponsorship—a person with similar experiences serves as a mentor or guide. In the case of homelessness, connecting a person presently experiencing homelessness with a support person who has had lived experience in the past seems like an element worth exploring. In addition, the regular meetings to hear stories, to interact with each other, and to provide support could prove to be a useful model for those experiencing homelessness. The final element is a combination of being responsible and being of service. A person with lived experience can be of direct service to someone currently without a home or to someone just finding housing. This type of network building, community building, has real promise.

One of the important features of these programs is that their proliferation has had a substantial impact on reducing the stigma attached to the various conditions to which they are addressed. Because of AA and NA, open discussion of alcoholism and drug addiction is much more prevalent now than it was fifty years ago. Once again, this is *not* suggesting that homelessness is tantamount to developmental disabilities or struggling with alcohol or substance use in any sense of the word. However, if creating supporters and regular meetings is a way of defusing negative stereotypes, maybe the organizational model should be considered.

Changing Public Perception and Mobilizing the Masses

One of the most significant aspects of our failure to end homelessness consists of the unfortunate misunderstandings by the general public about the issue, due mostly to misinformation and unsubstantiated stereotypes. In general, the public (1) typecasts homelessness to a narrow experience, characterizing the homeless as people who are unmotivated, have issues with substance use, or suffer some severe mental illness; (2) is aghast when they learn the issue is so much broader, specifically that it encompasses over a million school-aged children and their families; (3) once informed on the issue, wants to make an impact but has very little direction on how to meaningfully use this energy.

In order to change attitudes and misperceptions and eliminate the unsubstantiated stereotypes, we need a national public outreach campaign, like Mothers Against Drunk Driving—a campaign in the 1980s and 1990s to heighten awareness of the potential for major automobile accidents, usually fatal, in cases of drunk driving—or the movement about marriage equality, to get people's attention. We must take more initiative in creating ways to change public attitudes. Also, the campaign will be much stronger if we reach out to issue areas that are related to homelessness and engage them in meaningful partnerships. These areas include health, public benefits, education, hunger, childcare, and transportation. We need to mobilize various, but related, organizations to come together to strategize how to change policy and programs, commonly referred to as community organizing or building a political constituency.

A shift in the public perception of the issue must be the primary goal of a major campaign. People have to care about homelessness, recognize that it is not the result of personal character flaws, and start standing up for those who do not have a voice. In the digital age, there is ample opportunity to create this sort of public awareness campaign. One only needs to consider the widespread effects of the #MeToo campaign in bringing awareness to the issue of sexual harassment and assault. For the first time, victims felt empowered to begin coming forward regarding their experiences, demonstrating the depth of the issue, removing the stigma and shame, and changing the entire conversation about sexual harassment and assault. During Parkland, social media played a critical role in creating a grassroots movement against gun violence in our nation. As the shooting occurred, unlike in previous attacks, students streamed video of the actual attack, making it so much more concrete for the millions watching. Social media also allowed for the large-scale organization of protests and walkouts at schools across the nation in its wake.

We certainly *do not* aim to equate sexual assault, gun violence, and homelessness. Rather, the crux of this discussion is that movements can be created. In the digital age, public perception can begin to change and widespread awareness can be created with a simple #hashtag. Storytelling can occur online, providing insight and a platform to change public perception, if we will just give those experiencing homelessness the time and space to do so and acknowledge the critical importance of listening.

Once people become more aware of the issue and have a greater understanding of its complexity and nuances, there must be a call to action. A social movement is important, but equally important is doing something. Several of our contributors are taking action. Leanne, after her experience, works tirelessly in the compassion industry. She is leading the charge to build affordable housing units, partnering with the faith community to do so, in an effort to offer real, lasting solutions to unstably housed individuals and families.

James, Michelle, and Marie also work and volunteer in this space. They are unique as they bring the voices of lived experience to this work, something that James argues is critical for ensuring that communities offer the appropriate supports.

A Call to Action: An Increased Emphasis on Networks and Community

While many of us cannot dedicate our lives to this issue, there are ways each of us can make an impact. An important first step is to start using person-first language. There is increasing recognition of the value in referring to some people as "individuals with disabilities" or "individuals with substance abuse disorders"; this person-first language should be applied in the realm of homelessness. We should shift the language to a "person experiencing homelessness" or someone with "lived experience" versus continuing to use the outdated and somewhat derogatory term "homeless person." By changing the language in this way, we are saying that homelessness is a situation or a condition, rather than a personal attribute or personal flaw. This simple shift in language helps to break down stereotypes and change the perception of this issue, particularly if one is an individual with lived experience.

Person-first language is a stepping-stone in building public will; however, it is not the ultimate solution. Simply calling this issue by another name does not make it go away. There are other possible ways to have an impact. Be a part of a network that supports individuals living without a home or those at risk of losing their home. Let your legislators know you care about this issue and the necessary reforms in areas such as access to affordable housing, child welfare, criminal justice, eviction prevention, health care, and others established by this book's contributors, thus beginning a movement to change some of the systemic causes of homelessness.

If you have the time, volunteer somewhere locally. If you do not have the time to volunteer, but money is your gift, find a local organization and support it. This country needs more organizations to impact those without homes by providing networks of support and building communities. Be part of their support. Finally, get to know someone who is currently experiencing homelessness or has done so in the past. By engaging with individuals on a direct and personal basis, you will be transformed and come away with a totally different perception of what homelessness is.

It remains true that most services for those experiencing homelessness focus very little if any attention on increasing human resources for them. To repeat what Kevin Adler said, "These basic needs are essential to human survival. But we humans are complex. We also need to feel a sense of belonging, self-esteem, and love. These social supports are crucial for preventing—and exiting—homelessness" (K. Adler, personal communication, January 15, 2018).

If we are to be more successful in addressing homelessness, we must focus more energy on networks of support and on building community. Instead of focusing all our efforts on housing and services for each individual person experiencing homelessness, we must pay more attention to developing what the Australian Doorway program calls natural supports, human relationships, and interactions with others. Caring individuals, natural networks of support, and community are essential elements in helping people without homes become more self-sufficient and productive members of our society. As part of this emphasis shift, we must focus more attention on how to expand the choices available to those we are serving and to ensure their active participation in determining which option to choose.

Someone once asked, will we ever truly end homelessness? Our answer is that there will always be some individuals and families who end up without their homes for a period; that is unavoidable. However, what we can do is make sure that this is a rare occurrence, that no one is in that position for more than a month or two, and that after that hiatus, they will find a home of their own and remain stably housed. That, we think, is ultimately doable, if we have the political and collective will to accomplish it.

References

Abro, J. (2011). *An American Yoga: The Kripalu story.* New York, NY: Aerodale Press.

Administration for Children and Families. (n.d.) ACF's two-generation approach. Retrieved from https://www.acf.hhs.gov/sites/default/files/assets /acf_two_gen_flyer.pdf.

Agans, R. P., Liu, G., Jones, M., Verian, C., Silverbush, M., & Kalsbeek, W. D. (2011). Public attitudes toward the homeless. Paper presented at the 66th Annual Conference of the American Association for Public Opinion Research, Phoenix, AZ.

Alston, P. (2018, May). *Report of the special rapporteur on extreme poverty and human rights on his mission to the United States of America.* New York, NY: UN General Assembly.

American Psychological Association. (2018). Effects of poverty, hunger and homelessness on children and youth. Retrieved from https://www.apa.org/pi /families/poverty.aspx.

American Psychological Association, Presidential Task Force on Psychology's Contribution to End Homelessness. (2009). *Helping people without homes: The role of psychologists and recommendations to advance research, training, practice, and policy.* Retrieved from http://www.apa.org/pi/ses/resources /publications/end-homelessness.aspx.

Annie E. Casey Foundation. (2012). Stepping up for kids: What government and communities should do to support kinship families. Retrieved from https:// www.aecf.org/m/resourcedoc/AECF-SteppingUpForKids-2012.pdf.

The Aspen Institute, Ascend. (2014). Voices for two-generation success: Opportunities for policy change. Retrieved from https://ascend.aspeninstitute.org /wp-content/uploads/2017/10/Polling_tips_printing_lowres.pdf.

Avery, B., & Hernandez, P. (2018). Ban the box: U.S. cities, counties and states adopt fair hiring policies. National Employment Law Project. Retrieved from https://www.nelp.org/publication/ban-the-box-fair-chance-hiring-state -and-local-guide/.

Baum, A., & Burnes, D. (1993). *A nation in denial: The truth about homelessness.* Boulder, CO: Westview Press.

Baumohl, J. (1996). *Homelessness in America.* Washington, DC: Oryx for the National Coalition on Homelessness.

Beckett, K., & Herbert, S. (2009). *Banished: The new social control in urban America.* New York, NY: Oxford University Press.

Bellah, R., Madsen, R., Sullivan, A., & Tipton, S. (1985). *Habits of the heart.* Berkeley, CA: University of California Press.

Bivens, J., & Shierholz, H. (2018). *What labor market changes have generated inequality and wage suppression?* Economic Policy Institute Report. Retrieved from https://www.epi.org/publication/what-labor-market-changes-have-generated -inequality-and-wage-suppression-employer-power-is-significant-but-largely -constant-whereas-workers-power-has-been-eroded-by-policy-actions/.

Blau, J. (1992). *The visible poor: Homelessness in the United States.* New York, NY: Oxford University Press.

Board of Governors of the Federal Reserve System. (2017). *Report of the economic well-being of the U.S. households in 2016.* Retrieved from https:// www.federalreserve.gov/publications/files/2016-report-economic-well-being -us-households-201705.pdf.

Bredesen, D. (2016). Inhalation Alzheimer's disease: An unrecognized—and treatable—epidemic. *Aging, 8*(2), 304–313.

Burnes Center on Poverty and Homelessness, University of Denver. (2016). *An assessment of Adams County's efforts to address homelessness.* Retrieved from http://www.adcogov.org/sites/default/files/Adams%20Homelessness %20Assessment.pdf.

Burnes Center on Poverty and Homelessness, University of Denver. (2018). *Beloved community evaluation: April 2018.* Denver, CO: Author.

Burnes, D. (2019, March). Powerpoint presentation at Homelessness Summit, University of Maryland School of Social Work. Unpublished.

Burnes, D., & DiLeo, D. L. (Eds.). (2016). *Ending homelessness: Why we haven't, how we can.* Boulder, CO: Lynne Rienner Publishers.

Cain, T. (2014). *Healing Neen: One woman's path to salvation from trauma and addiction.* Deerfield Beach, FL: Health Communications.

California Family Resource Center Learning Circle. (2000). Vehicles for change, Vol. I, produced by Family Resource Center, April.

Centers for Disease Control and Prevention, National Institute for Occupational Safety and Health. (2012). *Preventing occupational respiratory disease from exposures caused by dampness in office buildings, schools, and other non-industrial buildings.* (DHHS [NIOSH] Publication No. 2013-102). Retrieved from https://www.cdc.gov/niosh/docs/2013-102/pdfs/2013-102.pdf.

Chase-Lansdale, P., Eckrich Sommer, T., Sabol, T., Chor, E., Brooks-Gunn, J., Yoshikawa, H., . . . Morris, A. (2017). What are the effects of pairing Head Start services with children with career pathway training for parents? Retrieved from https://www.captulsa.org/uploaded_assets/pdf/CAP-Tulsa-impact-analysis _Blizzardh-2017.pdf.

Children's Bureau. (2018). Placement of children with relatives. Retrieved from https://www.childwelfare.gov/pubPDFs/placement.pdf.

Chocano, C. (2018, April 17). What good is "community" when someone else makes all the rules? *New York Times Magazine,* p. 14.

Clemens, E. V., Helm, H. M., Myers, K., Thomas, C., & Tis, M. (2017). The voices of youth formerly in foster care: Perspectives on educational attainment gaps. *Children and Youth Services Review, 79,* 65–77.

Clemens, E. V., Klopfenstein, K., Lalonde, T. L., & Tis, M. (2018). The effects of placement and school stability on academic growth trajectories of students in foster care. *Children and Youth Services Review, 87*, 86–94.

Clemens, E. V., Klopfenstein, K., Tis, M., & Lalonde, T. L. (2017). Educational stability policy and the interplay between child welfare placements and school moves. *Children and Youth Services Review, 83*, 209–217.

Collinson, R., Ellen, I. G., & Ludwig, J. (2015). Low-income housing policy. In Robert A. Moffitt (Ed.), *Economics of means-tested transfer programs in the United States* (Vol. 2). Chicago, IL: University of Chicago Press.

Council of Economic Advisers. (2018). *Expanding work requirements in non-cash welfare programs*. Retrieved from https://www.whitehouse.gov/wp-content /uploads/2018/07/Expanding-Work-Requirements-in-Non-Cash-Welfare -Programs.pdf.

Culhane, D., Metraux, S., & Hadley, T. (2002). Public service reductions associated with placement of homeless persons with severe mental illness in supportive housing. *Housing Policy Debate, 13*(1).

Denver Leadership Foundation. (n.d.). Website material. Retrieved from http:// www.denverleadershipfoundation.com/models.htm.

Desmond, M. (2016). *Evicted.* New York, NY: Broadway Books.

de Tocqueville, A. ([1835] 1961). *Democracy in America.* New York, NY: Schocken.

Diaz, J., & Piña, G. (2013). Return on investment in the Jeremiah program. Retrieved from https://www.wilder.org/sites/default/files/imports/Jeremiah _ROI_REPORT_4-13.pdf.

Dworsky, A., Napolitano, L., & Courtney, M. E. (2013). Homelessness during the transition from foster care to adulthood. *American Journal of Public Health, 103*(Suppl. 2), S318–S323.

Economic Policy Institute. (2017). *The productivity-pay gap.* Retrieved from https://www.epi.org/productivity-pay-gap/.

Evans, W. N., Sullivan, J. X., & Wallskog, M. (2016). The impact of homelessness prevention programs on homelessness. *Science, 353*(6300), 694–699. Retrieved from http://science.sciencemag.org/content/353/6300/694.full.

Felitti, V. J., Anda, R. F., Nordenberg, D., Williamson, D. F., Spitz, A. M., Edwards, V., . . . Marks, J. S. (1998). Relationship of childhood abuse and household dysfunction to many of the leading causes of death in adults. *American Journal of Preventive Medicine, 14*(4), 245–258. doi:10.1016 /s0749-3797(98)00017-8.

Fowler, P., Toro, P., & Miles, B. (2009). Pathways to and from homelessness and associated psychosocial outcomes among adolescents leaving the foster care system. *American Journal of Public Health, 99*, 1453–1458.

Gallup. (2007). *Homelessness in America: Americans' perceptions, attitudes and knowledge.* Retrieved from https://shnny.org/uploads/2007_Gallup_Poll.pdf.

Garbarino, J. (1995). *Raising children in a socially toxic environment.* San Francisco, CA: Jossey-Bass.

George, S. (2018, May). *Enhancing homeless education and faculty engagement following the launch of the grand challenge to end homelessness: An evaluation study* (Unpublished doctoral dissertation). University of Southern California, Los Angeles.

Georgescu, P. (2017). *Capitalists arise!* Oakland, CA: Berrett-Koehler.

Gladwell, M. (2006, February 13). Million dollar Murray. *New Yorker Magazine,* p. 96.

Goldrick-Rab, S., Richardson, J., & Hernandez, A. (2017). *Hungry and homeless in college: Results from a national study of basic needs insecurity in higher education.* Retrieved from the University of Wisconsin's HOPE Lab website: http://wihopelab.com/publications/hungry-and-homeless-in-college-report.pdf.

Gordon, C. (2018). Growth (or not) in real wages. Economic Policy Institute. Retrieved from https://www.epi.org/blog/growth-or-not-in-real-wages/.

Gowan, T. (2010). *Hobos, hustlers, and backsliders: Homeless in San Francisco.* Minneapolis, MN: University of Minnesota Press.

Green, H., Tucker, J., Golinelli, D., & Wenzel, S. (2013). Social networks, time homeless, and social support. *Network Science, 1*(3), 305–320.

Grossman, J. B., & Rhodes, J. E. (2002). The test of time: Predictors and effects of duration in youth mentoring relationships. *PsycEXTRA Dataset.* doi:10 .1037/e314762004-001.

Groton, D., & Radey, M. (2018). Social network of unaccompanied women experiencing homelessness. *Journal of Community Psychology.* doi:10.1002 /jcop.22097.

Hardee, S., Sanford, G., & Burnes, D. (2019). Historic and current health care struggles for the homeless and skills for providers to improve care. *Archives of Family Medicine and General Practice, 4*(1), 77–81.

Hardin, B. (2016). Work, wages, wealth, and the roots of homelessness. In D. Burnes & D. L. DiLeo (Eds.), *Ending homelessness: Why we haven't, how we can.* Boulder, CO: Lynne Rienner Publishers.

Heben, A. (2014). *Tent city urbanism: From self-organized camps to tiny house villages.* Eugene, OR: The Village Collaborative.

Hines, S. (2018, May 27). How to prevent loss of a home. *Denver Post,* p. 4D.

Hoch, C., & Slayton, R. (1990). *New homeless and old: Community and the Skid Row Hotel.* Conflicts in Urban and Regional Development. Philadelphia, PA: Temple University Press.

Institute for College Access and Success. (2018). *Student debt and the class of 2017.* Retrieved from https://ticas.org/sites/default/files/pub_files/classof2017.pdf.

Jackson Nakazawa, D. (2015). 7 ways childhood adversity can change your brain. *Psychology Today.* Retrieved from https://www.psychologytoday.com/us/blog /the-last-best-cure/201508/7-ways-childhood-adversity-can-change-your-brain.

Jencks, C. (1994). *The Homeless.* Cambridge, MA: Harvard University Press.

Johnson, M. (2004). *Hull House.* Retrieved from http://www.encyclopedia .chicagohistory.org/pages/615.html.

Jones, J., Schmitt, J., & Wilson, V. (2018). 50 years after the Kerner commission: African Americans are better off in many ways but are still disadvantaged by racial inequality. Economic Policy Institute. Retrieved from https:// www.epi.org/publication/50-years-after-the-kerner-commission/.

Khadduri, J. (2016). Systems for homelessness and housing assistance. In D. W. Burnes & D. L. DiLeo (Eds.), *Ending homelessness: Why we haven't, how we can.* Boulder, CO: Lynne Rienner Publishers.

Kozol, J. (1987). *Rachel and her children: Homeless families in America.* New York, NY: Penguin.

Kusmer, K. (2002). *Down and out, on the road: The homeless in American history.* New York, NY: Oxford University Press.

Liebow, E. (1993). *Tell them who I am: The lives of homeless women.* New York, NY: Penguin.

Lutz, P., Tanti, A., Gasecka, A., Barnett-Burns, S., Kim, J. J., Zhou, Y., . . . Turecki, G. (2017). Association of a history of child abuse with impaired myelination in the anterior cingulate cortex: Convergent epigenetic, transcriptional, and morphological evidence. *American Journal of Psychiatry, 174*(12), 1185–1194. doi:10.1176/appi.ajp.2017.16111286.

McCoy, T. (2015). The surprisingly simple way Utah solved chronic homelessness and saved millions. *The Washington Post.* Retrieved from https://www.washingtonpost.com/news/inspired-life/wp/2015/04/17/the-surprisingly-simple-way-utah-solved-chronic-homelessness-and-saved-millions/?utm_term=.d69b8bcb3483.

McMillan, D. W., & Chavis, D. M. (1986). Sense of community: A definition and theory. *Journal of Community Psychology, 14.*

McNiel, D., Binder, R., & Robinson, J. (2005). Incarceration associated with homelessness, mental illness, and co-occurring substance use. *Psychiatric Services, 56*(7), 840–846.

Metraux, S., Roman, C., & Cho, R. (2007). Incarceration and homelessness. Paper presented at the 2007 National Symposium on Homelessness Research, Washington, DC.

Metro Denver Homeless Initiative. (2017). *Point-in-Time Report 2017.* Retrieved from https://d3n8a8pro7vhmx.cloudfront.net/mdhi/pages/12/attachments/original/1498599733/2017_Metro_Denver_PIT_Final.pdf?1498599733.

Miller, H. (1991). *On the fringe: The dispossessed in America.* Lexington, MA: Lexington Books.

Mullainathan, S., & Shafir, E. (2013). *Scarcity: The new science of having less and how it defines our lives.* New York, NY: Picador Books.

National Alliance to End Homelessness. (2013). *The state of homelessness in America 2013.* Retrieved from https://b.3cdn.net/naeh/bb34a7e4cd84ee985c_3vm6r7cjh.pdf.

National Alliance to End Homelessness. (2015). *The state of homelessness in America 2015: Trends in chronic homelessness.* Retrieved from https://endhomelessness.org/the-state-of-homelessness-in-america-2015-trends-in-chronic-homelessness/.

National Alliance to End Homelessness. (2016). Fact sheet: Housing first. Retrieved from http://endhomelessness.org/wp-content/uploads/2016/04/housing-first-fact-sheet.pdf.

National Alliance to End Homelessness. (2018a). *Chronically homeless.* Retrieved from https://endhomelessness.org/homelessness-in-america/who-experiences-homelessness/chronically-homeless/.

National Alliance to End Homelessness. (2018b). *Racial inequalities in homelessness, by the numbers.* Retrieved from https://endhomelessness.org/resource/racial-inequalities-homelessness-numbers/.

National Center for Education Statistics. (2017). *Digest of education statistics* (Table 204.75e). Retrieved from https://nces.ed.gov/programs/digest/d16/tables/dt16_204.75e.asp.

National Center for Homeless Education. (2017a). *Children and youth experiencing homelessness: An introduction to the issues.* Retrieved from https://nche.ed.gov/downloads/briefs/introduction.pdf.

National Center for Homeless Education. (2017b). *Federal data summary school years 2013–2014 to 2015–2016: Education for homeless children and youth.* Retrieved from https://nche.ed.gov/downloads/data-comp-1314-1516.pdf.

National Center for Homeless Education. (2017c). *Supporting the education of unaccompanied students experiencing homelessness.* Retrieved from https://nche.ed.gov/downloads/briefs/youth.pdf.

National Center for Homeless Education. (2018). *National overview.* Retrieved from https://www.nhchc.org/faq/official-definition-homelessness.

National Center for Homeless Education. (2019). *Federal data summary for school years 2014–15 to 2016–17.* Retrieved from https://nche.ed.gov

/wp-content/uploads/2019/02/Federal-Data-Summary-SY-14.15-to-16.17
-Final-Published-2.12.19.pdf.

National Conference of State Legislatures. (2016). Homeless and runaway youth. Retrieved from http://www.ncsl.org/research/human-services/homeless-and -runaway-youth.aspx.

National Conference of State Legislatures. (2018). Two-generation strategies toolkit. Retrieved from http://www.ncsl.org/research/human-services/two -generation-strategies-toolkit.aspx.

National Health Care for the Homeless Council. (2018). *What is the official definition of homelessness?* Retrieved from https://www.nhchc.org/faq/official -definition-homelessness.

National Housing Law Project. (2017). *Low-income housing tax credits.* Retrieved from https://www.nhlp.org/resource-center/low-income-housing-tax-credits.

National Law Center on Homelessness and Poverty. (2015). *Homelessness in America: Overview of data and causes.* Retrieved from https://www.nlchp .org/documents/Homeless_Stats_Fact_Sheet.

National Law Center on Homelessness and Poverty. (2017). *Housing not handcuffs.* Washington, DC: Author.

National Low Income Housing Coalition. (2018a). *The gap: A shortage of affordable homes.* Retrieved from http://nlihc.org/sites/default/files/Gap -Report_2017.pdf.

National Low Income Housing Coalition. (2018b). *How much do you need to earn to afford a modest apartment in your state?* Retrieved from http://nlihc.org/oor.

National Low Income Housing Coalition. (2018c) *Out of Reach: The High Cost of Housing.* Washington, DC: Author.

National Low Income Housing Coalition. (n.d.) *State and local housing trust funds.* Retrieved from http://nlihc.org/sites/default/files/2014AG-277.pdf.

Nous Group. (2014, February 3). *Doorway—Summative Evaluation—November 2013.* Retrieved from https://recoverylibrary.unimelb.edu.au/__data/assets /pdf_file/0019/1391302/doorway-summative_evaluation_report-final.pdf.

O'Brien, T. (2016). In pursuit of quality data and programs. In D. Burnes & D. L. DiLeo (Eds.), *Ending homelessness: Why we haven't, how we can.* Boulder, CO: Lynne Rienner Publishers.

Olivet, J., & Dones, M. (2017). Racial equity: An essential component of our nation's homelessness response system. US Interagency Council on Homelessness. Retrieved from https://www.usich.gov/news/racial-equity-an-essential -component-of-our-nations-homelessness-response.

Olivet, J., Dones, M., Richard, M., Wilkey, C., Yampolskaya, S., Beit-Arie, M., & Joseph, L. (2018). SPARC: Phase one study findings. Retrieved from the Center for Social Innovation website: http://center4si.com/wp-content/uploads /2018/03/SPARC-Phase-1-Findings-Blizzardh-20181.pdf.

Oxford House. (2018). *Annual Report: Fiscal Year 2017.* Silver Spring, MD. Retrieved from https://www.oxfordhouse.org/userfiles/file/doc/ar2017.pdf.

Pastore, A. L., & Maguire, K. (Eds.). (2005). *Sourcebook of criminal justice statistics.* Retrieved from the Hindelang Criminal Justice Center, University of Albany website: www.albany.edu/sourcebook/.

Polkinghorne, D. (2007). Validity issues in narrative research. *Qualitative Inquiry, 14*(4), 471–486. Retrieved from https://pdfs.semanticscholar.org /f87f/81aff20792f4e9332b96c24cd705b072eec7.pdf.

Pruitt, A. S., Barile, J. P., Ogawa, T. Y., Peralta, N., Bugg, R., Lau, J., & Mori, V. (2018). Housing First and photovoice: Transforming lives, communities, and systems. *American Journal of Community Psychology, 61*(1–2), 104–117. Retrieved from http://onlinelibrary.wiley.com/doi/10.1002/ajcp.12226/full.

Reisch, M. (2014). *Why macro practice matters.* Essay commissioned by the Special Commission to Advance Macro Practice in Social Work initiated by the Association of Community Organization and Social Administration, Livonia, MI.

Rollinson, P., & Pardeck, J. (2006). *Homelessness in rural America: Policy and practice.* New York, NY: Haworth Press.

Rossi, P. (1989). *Down and out in America: The origins of homelessness.* Chicago, IL: University of Chicago Press.

Rothman, J. (2013). *Education for macro intervention: A survey of problems and prospects.* Essay commissioned by the Association for Community Organization and Social Administration, Livonia, MI.

Rusch, E. (2016, June 1). Median price of one-bedroom apartment in Denver hit $1,390 in May. *Denver Post.* Retrieved from https://www.denverpost.com/2016/06/01/median-price-of-a-1br-apartment-in-denver-hit-1390-in-may/.

Ryan, W. (1976). *Blaming the victim.* New York, NY: Vintage Books.

Sekharan, V. (2016). Infographic: Adverse childhood experiences and adult homelessness. Retrieved from http://homelesshub.ca/blog/infographic-adverse-childhood-experiences-and-adult-homelessness.

Shah, M. F., Liu, Q., Mark Eddy, J., Barkan, S., Marshall, D., Mancuso, D., . . . Huber, A. (2017). Predicting homelessness among emerging adults aging out of foster care. *American Journal of Community Psychology, 60,* 33–43.

Snow, D. A., & Anderson, L. (1993). *Down on their luck: A study of homeless street people.* Berkeley, CA: University of California Press.

Sommeiller, E., & Price, M. (2018, July 19). The new gilded age: Income inequality in the U.S. by state, metropolitan area, and county. Economic Policy Institute. Retrieved from https://www.epi.org/publication/the-new-gilded-age-income-inequality-in-the-u-s-by-state-metropolitan-area-and-county/.

Stergiopoulos, V., Hwang, S. W., Gozdzik, A. Nisenbaum, R., Latimer, E., Rabouin, D., . . . Goering, P. (2015). Effects of scattered site housing using rent supplements and intensive case management on housing stability among homeless adults with mental illness: A randomized trial. *JAMA, 313*(9), 905–915. Retrieved from https://jamanetwork.com/journals/jama/fullarticle/2174029?linkid=12694817.

Sturm College of Law. (2016). *Too high a price: What criminalizing homelessness costs Colorado.* Denver, CO: University of Denver.

Sturm College of Law. (2018). *Too high a price—2.* Denver, CO: University of Denver.

Substance Abuse and Mental Health Services Administration. (2018). Adverse childhood experiences. Retrieved from https://www.samhsa.gov/capt/practicing-effective-prevention/prevention-behavioral-health/adverse-childhood-experiences.

Tobin, K., & Murphy, J. (2016). The new demographics of homelessness. In D. Burnes & D. L. DiLeo (Eds.), *Ending homelessness: Why we haven't, how we can.* Boulder, CO: Lynne Rienner Publishers.

Torres, K., & Mathur, R. (2018). Fact sheet: Family First Prevention Services Act. Retrieved from https://campaignforchildren.org/resources/fact-sheet/fact-sheet-family-first-prevention-services-act/.

Tsafrir, J. (2017, August 3). Mold toxicity: A common cause of psychiatric symptoms. *Psychology Today.* Retrieved from https://www.psychologytoday.com/us/blog/holistic-psychiatry/201708/mold-toxicity-common-cause-psychiatric-symptoms.

US Department of Health and Human Services. (2018). *Tick-borne disease working group.* Retrieved from https://www.hhs.gov/ash/advisory-committees/tickbornedisease/index.html.

US Department of Housing and Urban Development. (2012). *Home and CDBG: Working together to create housing—training manual and slides.* Retrieved

from https://www.hudexchange.info/resource/267/home-and-cdbg-working
-together-to-create-affordable-housing-training-manual/.

US Department of Housing and Urban Development. (2017a). *2017 Annual Homeless Assessment Report to Congress.* Washington, DC.

US Department of Housing and Urban Development. (2017b). *Coordinated entry policy brief.* Retrieved from https://www.hudexchange.info/resources/documents /Coordinated-Entry-Policy-Brief.pdf.

US Department of Housing and Urban Development. (2018). *Housing trust fund.* Retrieved from https://www.hudexchange.info/programs/htf/.

US Interagency Council on Homelessness. (2018a). *Ending veteran homelessness.* Retrieved from https://www.usich.gov/goals/veterans.

US Interagency Council on Homelessness. (2018b, September). *Homelessness in America: Focus on families with children.* Retrieved from https://www.usich .gov/resources/uploads/asset_library/Homeslessness_in_America_Families _with_Children.pdf.

US Interagency Council on Homelessness. (2018c). *Homelessness in America: Focus on youth.* Retrieved from https://www.usich.gov/tools-for-action/homelessness -in-america-focus-on-youth/.

Wagner, D. (2018). *No longer homeless.* Lanham, MD: Rowman & Littlefield.

Wasserman, J., & Clair, J. (2010). *At home on the street: People, poverty and a hidden culture of homelessness.* Boulder, CO: Lynne Rienner Publishers.

Wasserman, J., & Clair, J. (2016). Controversies in the provision of services. In D. Burnes & D. L. DiLeo (Eds.), *Ending homelessness: Why we haven't, how we can.* Boulder, CO: Lynne Rienner Publishers.

Western Regional Advocacy Project. (2006). *Without housing: Decades of federal housing cutbacks, massive homelessness and policy failures.* San Francisco, CA.

Whelley, C., & McCabe, C. (2016). Rights, responsibilities, and homelessness. In D. Burnes & D. L. DiLeo (Eds.), *Ending homelessness: Why we haven't, how we can.* Boulder, CO: Lynne Rienner Publishers.

Williams, J. (2003). *A roof over my head: Homeless women and the shelter industry.* Louisville, CO: University Press of Colorado.

Wilson, W. (1987). *The truly disadvantaged: The inner city, the underclass, and public policy.* Chicago, IL: University of Chicago Press.

Wissman, L. (2017). 2017 federal poverty level guidelines. *People Keep.* Retrieved from https://www.peoplekeep.com/blog/2017-federal-poverty-level-guidelines.

Wright, J. (1989). *Address unknown: The homeless in America.* New York, NY: Walter de Gruyter.

Yang, A. (2018). *The war on normal people: The truth about America's disappearing jobs and why universal basic income is our future.* New York, NY: Hachette Books.

Index

About the Book

How do individuals move from being homeless to finding safe, stable, and secure places to live? Can we recreate the conditions that helped them most? What policies are needed to support what worked—and to remove common obstacles?

Addressing these questions, Jamie Rife and Donald Burnes start from the premise that the most important voices in efforts to end homelessness are the ones most often missing from the discussion: the voices of those with lived experience. In *Journeys Out of Homelessness*, they gather the first-person stories of some who have not only survived, but thrived, going on to find positive home situations.

Highlighting what we can learn from these personal stories, Rife and Burnes combine them with in-depth discussions of key themes and issues and point to the shifts necessary in current policy and practice that are essential if we are to effectively respond to a problem that has reached epic proportions.

Jamie Rife is cofounder and head of operations at Purposity, a nonprofit crowd-funding platform that fosters the creation of online networks of support for individuals dealing with poverty and homelessness. **Donald W. Burnes** is founder of and adviser to the Burnes Center on Poverty and Homelessness at the University of Denver Graduate School of Social Work.